BASEBALL'S
FORGOTTEN
HEROES

BASEBALL'S FORGOTTEN HEROES

One Fan's Search for the Game's
Most Interesting Overlooked Players

TONY SALIN

𝓂𝓅
MASTERS PRESS

NTC/Contemporary Publishing Group

Library of Congress Cataloging-in-Publication Data

Salin, Tony.
    Baseball's forgotten heroes : one fan's search for the game's most interesting overlooked players / Tony Salin ; foreword by Peter Golenbock.
        p.   cm.
    ISBN 0-8092-2603-0
    1. Baseball players—United States—Biography. 2. Baseball players—United States—Interviews. 3. Baseball—United States—History. 4. Salin, Tony. I. Title.
GV865.A1S245   1999
795.357'092'273
[b]—dc21   98-41463
                                                  CIP

Sources for statistical information include *Minor League Baseball Stars* (Vol. 1, 2, 3), *Nineteenth Century Stars,* and *The Negro Leagues Book* by the Society for American Baseball Research, Cleveland, Ohio; *The Baseball Encyclopedia; Total Baseball;* and various editions of *The Baseball Register.*

Cover photograph copyright © Myron/Tony Stone Images
Cover design by Nick Panos
Interior design by Impressions Book and Journal Services, Inc.

Published by Masters Press
A division of NTC/Contemporary Publishing Group, Inc.
4255 West Touhy Avenue, Lincolnwood (Chicago), Illinois 60646-1975 U.S.A.
Copyright © 1999 by Tony Salin
Printed in the United States of America
International Standard Book Number: 0-8092-2603-0
99 00 01 02 03 04 QP 18 17 16 15 14 13 12 11 10 9 8 7 6 5 4 3 2 1

To my Sacramento friends, especially Randy E. Marx, Jeni Rund, Jan Darvas, Adrien Korchmaros-Hallabrin, Karen Cohen (and her two sons, Aaron and Dan), and a group of people someone really should write about, the drivers from Capitol City Co-Op Cab. More than anyone else, I dedicate this book to my longtime friend Debbie Rund Caldwell. To the others I met in Sacramento through the years, "hello!"

At the request of the author, 20 percent of the royalties from the sale of this book will be sent to the American Red Cross for use in disaster-relief services.

Contents

FOREWORD

I get calls from people all the time who want to write books. Most of them have excellent ideas. I've heard from writers who wish to publish biographies of players like Honus Wagner and even from former players who wish to write their own stories. Unfortunately, in this age of disappearing history, it is almost impossible to get a book published if you haven't published one already, and it is rare that I can do much of anything to help. The shame of it is that most baseball fans aren't much interested in the game's history. And that's too bad because in no other sport do we find such a rich collection of wonderful characters and stories. It's why I've spent the last 20 years of my life writing about it.

About a year ago, I got a call from Tony Salin who was living out in San Francisco. Tony informed me that he drives a taxicab for a living, and he said that the day before he had picked up a doctor friend of mine from Boston, and they began discussing a book Tony was in the middle of writing. The doctor, who I've known for many years, had given Tony my number.

I was enchanted by that first call because, for 10 minutes, all Tony talked about was the books I had written, and it's the dream of every writer to get phone calls from strangers who gush on about how wonderful your work is. Don't let anyone kid you—sucking up really works. After Tony finished salaaming, he began talking about the book he was working on, a wonderful project that allowed him to interview a disparate group of ex-major and -minor league baseball players whose lives had fascinated him because of something they had done during their careers. He mentioned interviewing the legendary Unser Choe Hauser, who twice hit 60 home runs in a season. He talked about stories he'd uncovered regarding ballplayer-turned-actor Chuck Connors and recounted his conversation with the reclusive

Pete Gray, the only player in the history of the major leagues ever to play a fielding position despite the handicap of having only one arm.

"You actually got to speak to Pete?" I asked. Tony said he had and described the conversation. I was enthralled, for Pete Gray has long been a character I've had great interest in knowing something about. How did he get his first job in baseball? How did he lose his arm? Gray had told Tony some priceless stories and so, it turned out, had a whole wonderful collection of baseball's old-timers.

I have always been drawn to enthusiasm. Life to me is passion. I have always felt sorry for people who had no hobbies or passions, no matter how offbeat. I have a friend who loves his collection of lawn sprinklers from around the world. It's what makes him happy. My friend Barry Halper collects baseball memorabilia to the point that it has taken over his life. It has *become* his life, and he is enriched for it. Tony Salin's passion, I am happy to say, is collecting baseball memories, not necessarily from the stars who have told their stories over and over, but from the men who played beside the stars and from men who were fortunate enough to spend their lives roaming the small towns of America playing the game of baseball.

If I did one thing for Tony Salin, it was to encourage him to reveal more of himself in his book. He added personal stories about his encounters with the players as well as the details of the detective work he undertook to track them down.

Tony has an instinct. He knows what he wants to know and knows who to ask to get it. His subjects played with and against the best players in memory: Babe Ruth, Lou Gehrig, Ty Cobb, Grover Cleveland Alexander, Rogers Hornsby, Jackie Robinson, Dizzy Dean, Lefty Grove, Hack Wilson, Satchel Paige, Joe DiMaggio, Ted Williams, and Mickey Mantle. They played in the majors, and they played in the tank towns, the minor league havens like Roswell, New Mexico, where one season Joe Bauman hit 72 home runs, and Three Rivers, Canada, where Pete Gray got his start. They played in Mexico, in the Caribbean, and in Japan. But regardless of where they played, what they have in common is they played with baseball in their hearts, and that's what Tony Salin brings to this book as much as anything else. I hope you enjoy this journey into the kingdom of baseball as much as I did.

—Peter Golenbock

Acknowledgments

I worked on this book between 1991 and 1998. Many people assisted me and I sincerely hope that all of them realize how much I appreciate their efforts.

First and foremost, I want to thank Peter Golenbock, the gifted writer who took me under his wing. Peter made phone calls for me, gave me advice whenever I asked, and reminded me by his actions that there are some really decent people out there. Thank you, Peter. May you play softball until you're 90.

Besides Peter Golenbock, without whose help this book may not have been published, I will eternally be grateful to Andy Epstein for putting me in touch with Peter, and to Ken Samelson, my editor.

Writers Ed Beitiks, Bob Broeg, and Jack B. Moore made major contributions to this book (mainly because I asked and they were too generous by nature to say no).

For advice on a variety of issues and encouragement, I have many to thank, especially Dave Barlow, Rick Parmer, Jack Bedard, Stephanie Ingrahm, Tom "Gus" Semple, Debbie Rund Caldwell, Brian Zevnik, Rick Wolff, Jim Charlton, Karen Cohen, Mark Alvarez, Dan Kinion, Janet Spires, Randy R. Mitchell, Tom McIntyre, John Spalding, Jacqueline Marilyn Ivens, Chris Shaub, Seang "Justin" Truong, Cassandra Lynn, Tim Holt, Madgolene Mogyorosi, my brothers Doug and George Salin and sister Patricia Huston, and Kevin Kerrane. (If you haven't read Kevin's book *Dollar Sign on the Muscle*, you've missed a true baseball classic.)

Special thanks are due my friend David Nemec, whose *Great Baseball Feats, Facts and Firsts* was invaluable in my early research.

Along with original interviews, the backbone of this book came in the form of bits of information gleaned from newspapers located in over 60 libraries in the United States and Canada. My indebtedness to librarians and appreciation for their efforts is immense. Some of the librarians who helped with research included Enid Hanks, Beverly Lane, Barb Hastings, Virginia Holsten, Ron Davenport, Diane Tufts, Mary Ann Pirone, Kathy Jones, Greta Stephenson, Karen L. Graff, Beth Patterson, Kathryne French, Stephanie Clark, Alex S. Weinbaum, Roberta Dewing, Judith Lasher-Tidwell, Jean Gillmer, Helen Fleming, Jan Hildebrand, Steve Lavoie, Elaine Stefanko, Mark Allnatt, Joan McKinnie, George Schroeter, Judith Walsh, Joan Annsfire, Mary Gonella, Jeff Korman, Jean Missud, Nancy Gaudette, Elvis Fleming, Lea Frazier, Michael Salmon, and Walter Kurth.

Baseball Hall of Fame staff members who assisted with research included Timothy Rogers, Matt Washburn, Gary Van Allen, Dan Cunningham, Julie Johnson, Matt Reese, W. C. "Bill" Burdick, and Bill Deane.

My unofficial, but highly skilled photo editor—and fellow cabdriver—Rich Koury, was a tremendous help, as were the following people who contributed in various ways: Walter Langford, Mary Brace, Lew Lipset, Julia Anderson, James B. Davidson, Steve Stevens, Bill Lange Jr., and Kye Rorie IV.

Naturally, I owe a great debt to the ballplayers I interviewed. They all were gracious, honest, and generous with their time. I enjoyed talking with all of them, from the joke tellers to the serious ones, from the ribald to the reserved.

Some people whom I've never met but feel a deep gratitude to include Bob Hoie, Ray Nemec, Bob Davids, Bob McConnell, and others who have spent an incredible amount of time over the years digging for retired players' biographical information and compiling complete career records. These true lovers of baseball are all members of The Society for American Baseball Research, generally known as SABR. SABR, which is open to everyone—not just researchers—can be reached at (216) 575-0500.

Morris Eckhouse of SABR once said, "There's a whole galaxy of players waiting to be discovered," which is what this book is about. Many of baseball's most interesting stories concern players who are all but unknown to most fans. What I've tried to do with this book is help more fans tap into that unlimited supply of stories and players.

BASEBALL'S FORGOTTEN HEROES

The Most Amazing Player Ever

PETE GRAY

When I hear people mention Pete Gray, they usually say something like, "Yeah, the one-armed guy. Played during World War II when the good players were away." There always seems to be something negative about it—a rub, a put-down. I see Pete Gray differently. For me, he is perhaps the most extraordinary player who ever lived. He didn't excel on the major league level, but the argument could be made that if all professional ballplayers were ranked on ability and value, Pete Gray would be grouped in the top 50 percent. A one-armed pool player OK, a one-armed tennis player maybe, but a one-armed baseball player who could play at that level—that's absolutely remarkable.

Pete Gray is known as a recluse. Years ago he had his phone disconnected, and I have read that he won't even answer his door if he thinks it might be a writer. Every once in a while he grants an interview, but it's rare.

I knew there was only a slim chance he would respond, but I wrote him a letter and told him I was working on a book. I was especially interested in getting a firsthand account of Gray's entry into pro ball. I told him I thought he was a much better ballplayer than most people realized and asked him to please call me collect. Much to my surprise, a few days after I sent the letter, he called.

"I hardly ever call anybody," he said. "So what did you really want to know?"

We talked for about half an hour. He was cordial, but he kept trying to get off the phone. "Hey, I'm going to Scranton. Those guys are waiting for me." He said he and some pals were driving to Scranton to watch a friend in a pool tournament. But I was talking to the one and only Pete Gray, and I didn't want to stop. I threw him more questions, and he kept responding. A few times it sounded like somebody hit the clicker on the phone and I also heard what sounded like the rotary dial being spun. Still I pressed on, and he kept talking.

Our conversation took place early in 1992. I liked him. His story starts with an explanation of how he lost his arm.

PETE GRAY: I was six or seven years old when a huckster come into town. He was selling stuff—you know, potatoes and apples—and he said he'd give me a quarter or something if I'd go house-to-house and tell them about the potatoes and apples. After he was done, he was leaving town, and I was on the running board, and he said, "Jump off." And I slipped—in those days trucks had wooden spokes, and my arm caught in the spokes.

He picked me up and brought me home and set me on the porch. Then a lady was walking by and she saw I was bleeding and so she called a doctor, and they come over for me and took me to the hospital. Well, they cut my arm off that night. I stayed in the hospital for 10 to 15 days. To tell you the truth, I don't remember exactly, because I was too young.

Growing up in Nanticoke we had a baseball team on our street, and I was better than any of them. We played other streets. I knew I was pretty good, and later on I went to Hot Springs, Arkansas, to a baseball school. Ray Doan owned the school, and he called all over the country to get me on a Class D club, and they thought there was something wrong with him, you know. They thought he was crazy. He tried, anyhow, and he kept me there for 10 days, paid my expenses and everything, and then I came home. He said he couldn't do nothing for me.

Then in 1938 I was playing for a team in Pennsylvania, four days a week, and there was a player by the name of Skelton. He went to Three Rivers, Canada, and they wanted an outfielder up there. So he called me up and told me to meet the manager in Montreal, at the train station. But Skelton didn't tell them that I had one arm. And I didn't know that.

At the train station there was a fellow walking with a suitcase and he had a bat on the side of the suitcase. The manager went up to him and said, "Gray," but the guy thought he said, "Say," or something, and they shook hands. So the manager thought that guy was me, and he said, "Well, we've got to catch the train." So we're on the train, and he was talking about baseball to that guy. We found out later that he was a softball player.

A little before Three Rivers that guy got up to get off the train, and the manager says, "No, you're not getting off here. We're playing tonight in Three Rivers." He said, "No, I'm playing here." And the manager looked at me and he says, "What's your name?" I said, "Gray." Well, he says, "What's the matter with your arm?"

"I don't have any."

"Jesus," he said. "Say that again. What's your name?"

"Gray."

He said, "What are you coming here for?"

"To play ball."

"Who sent you here?"

"A guy by the name of Skelton."

"Oh," he says. "I'm in trouble."

The next stop was Three Rivers, and we got off and the owners were there—you know, the directors—and one of them came up to me and said, "You're a ballplayer? With one arm?"

I said, "Yeah."

Well, anyhow, when we came to the ballpark, they wouldn't give me a suit or nothing. But the game started, and the first guy for Quebec came up and hit a home run. And that's how that ball game went. In the middle of the game one of the directors told me to put a uniform on. So the clubhouse boy gave me a uniform, and I put it on.

Well, anyhow, they used all the batters and the pitcher was the last hitter, with two out and the bases loaded in the last inning. So the manager says to me, "Gray, go up there and hit." The batter had one strike on him before the manager put me in. So I come out of the dugout swinging two bats, you know, around. And you could have heard a pin drop.

Well, anyhow, I got a base hit, and we won the ball game. And the people started throwing change on the field. They gave me a check for over five hundred dollars. So that was something. It was like a guy wrote a book or something.

After that I played with the Bushwicks and Bay Parkways in New York.

Gray was such a novelty that the July 29, 1940, issue of Newsweek had a picture of him in his Bay Parkway uniform. The short article mentioned that "Pete Gray . . . now plays center field for the Bay Parkways, semipro team in Brooklyn, not because of his box-office value as a curiosity but because he is really an asset. Up to last week he had accepted 34 chances without an error and, as leadoff man in the lineup, he was batting a lofty .449."

When Three Rivers got in Organized Baseball in 1942, they knew what I could do, so they sent me a contract. From there they sold me to Toronto, on the "look basis." We were supposed to play the Philadelphia Athletics in an exhibition game. I got sick and couldn't go, and they released me. I always had trouble with owners—contracts, you know. Maybe they thought I was a bad guy. I don't know.

Well, the papers picked it up. It went all over the country that I was released by Toronto. Mickey O'Neil, my manager from Three Rivers, was in Memphis at that time, and he went in and talked with Doc Prothro, the manager and part owner of the Memphis club. And Mickey O'Neil told him, "Get that guy." Prothro told Mickey, "You must be going nuts or something." But anyway, in about four days he sent me a check and he told me to come out to Memphis. That was in 1943. I was there 1943 and '44. I had a good year in '44. I was voted the Most Valuable Player in the Southern Association. [Gray hit .333 in 1944 and tied a league record with 68 stolen bases.]

I was a pretty good hitter. And I was a good bunter, too. Center field was my position. I could cover a lot of ground in the outfield. And if I touched the ball, I caught it. I had a pretty good arm, up until 1942, when I broke my collarbone. That sort of held me back a little. I could still throw, but not like I used to.

In 1944 Doc Prothro told me I was going to go to the big leagues the next year. He didn't know if it would be with the Giants or the St. Louis Browns. He thought it would be the Browns, because Memphis had a working agreement with them.

Pete Gray (© *Brace Photo*)

I knew I wouldn't be up there too long. When I got there I was too old, 30 years old. I was hitting the ball good, but my average wasn't too good. They couldn't strike me out, you know. I only struck out nine or ten times in 77 games. They started me off in left field and after a while they put me in center field. I played center field all my life.

The Browns sent me to Toledo in 1946 and I played in about half the games. One day I had seven for seven, in a doubleheader. Four for four in the first game, three for three in the second game. In the second game we were behind two to one in the ninth inning, and the first batter popped up. The next guy come up hit a triple, and we were behind a run and I was the next batter. So they took the pitcher

out and put a left-hander in to pitch against me. So Don Gutteridge—
he was our manager—he took me out and put another guy in, and
that guy popped up. That was two out, and we had a fellow by the
name of Jerry Witte, and he hit one out. So we beat them anyway.
But I went seven for seven. Wasn't that something? That only happens once in a lifetime.

*Gray sat out the 1947 season, and in 1948 he played for Elmira in the East-
ern League. In 1949 he played for Dallas in the Texas League, and then he
barnstormed for a while with the House of David team, a team known best for
the beards its players wore.*

I didn't grow a beard, but the other guys had them. We had a two-
month schedule, and we carried our own lights. We used to put
them up wherever we played, like a carnival. We'd take them down
and go to the next town. I didn't care where I played, you know, just
as long as I had a uniform on. That's all I wanted. I think I was a
pretty good ballplayer. I'd say I was a good Triple A player.

I really enjoyed that season with the Browns. It would have been
better if I had gone up a little earlier, when I was younger. But I
always wanted to play in Yankee Stadium, and I finally made it. I
was 30 when I reached the majors in '45. I'm a little older than some
of the books say. My manager said I should say I was a little
younger. I was born in 1915. I'm 77 now.

When I played baseball, it was a long time ago.

Roman Bertrand on Pete Gray

*Roman Bertrand played against Pete Gray in 1938 in Canada's Provincial
League—a league not affiliated with Organized Baseball. Bertrand, whose
nickname was Lefty, recalls his surprise at the talent of baseball's only one-
armed ballplayer.*

LEFTY BERTRAND: Pete Gray? Yes, I pitched against him. He hit a
triple off the right field wall off of me. One-handed. And that fence
was about 340 feet. He was a left-handed hitter, you know, and he got
wood on that ball. He hit way over .300 in that outlaw league, and
that was a pretty good league. That was equivalent to, oh, I would say

Baseball's one-armed wonder, Pete Gray, pulling a ball to right in a 1945 game against the Yankees. Gray was an all-star in the minors, batting .333 for the Memphis Chicks in 1944 while tying a Southern Association record that year with 68 stolen bases. (*AP/Wide World Photos*)

Class A, at that time. It got to be real good. I can't remember the names, but there were several former big league players in that league. They were getting more money there than they would be getting playing down in the minor leagues. That's the reason I went there.

We heard there was a one-armed ballplayer coming in, and we thought, "This must be some league, hiring one-armed ballplayers." I faced him in two ball games. I thought that I wouldn't have any trouble with him. But I had a little trouble with him. I tell you, he could run. And he would drag bunt a lot. He'd bunt that ball down the third base line, and the third baseman had to be playing right up there or he'd never get him. Then he'd push one back by the pitcher—he was a pretty smart ballplayer.

In the field he had a great arm—a shotgun arm. He'd catch that ball in his glove, and he'd flip it up in the air, and put his glove under his stub arm, and then he'd catch the ball, coming down, and then throw it in the same motion. It was amazing. No telling what he would have done if he'd had two hands.

I'm glad I played against him. It doesn't happen very often that you're facing a one-armed ballplayer.

Pete Gray (real name: Peter J. Wyshner)

Born March 6, 1915, Nanticoke, PA.
Batted left, threw left. Height: 6' 1". Weight: 169 lbs.

Year	Club	League	Position	G	AB	R	H	2B	3B	HR	RBI	SB	BA
1938	Three Rivers	+Provincial	OF	—	60	7	17	0	0	1	8	—	.283
1939–41							(independent teams)						
1942	Three Rivers	Can.-Am.	OF	42	160	31	61	5	0	0	13	5	.381
1943	Memphis	Southern	OF	126	453	56	131	7	6	0	42	13	.289
1944	Memphis	Southern	OF	129	501	119	167	21	9	5	60	68*	.333
1945	St. Louis	American	OF	77	234	26	51	6	2	0	13	5	.218
1946	Toledo	American Assn.	OF	48	96	14	24	3	0	0	7	2	.250
1947							(voluntarily retired)						
1948	Elmira	Eastern	OF	82	269	37	78	7	2	0	14	5	.290
1949	Dallas	Texas	OF	45	56	18	12	2	0	0	5	5	.214
	Major League totals			77	234	26	51	6	2	0	13	5	.218
	Minor League totals			472	1595	282	490	45	17	6	149	98	.307

+ Not affiliated with organized baseball

* Led league

2

Now Batting for Furillo, the "Rifleman"

CHUCK CONNORS

When I first began formulating the idea for this book, before I knew if I was going to begin it, I tried to contact Chuck Connors, but failed. He died shortly thereafter, in 1992, from lung cancer. He was a smoker; his illness was of short duration.

What I've learned since about Chuck Connors boggles me. To say that his life was full is an understatement of huge proportions. Connors was intense, complex, and, I believe, one of the most driven individuals this planet has ever seen.

Known primarily for his portrayal of warm but tough homesteader Lucas McCain on TV's The Rifleman, *Connors had an acting career broader than most people realize, and a career in baseball that will surprise those not familiar with his past. Connors was a personality who quite possibly will be forgotten by future generations—and that would be a shame, because Chuck Connors was a wonderful, likable maniac—a unique guy, a presence.*

Kevin Joseph Aloysius "Chuck" Connors was the talk of the 1949 Brooklyn Dodgers training camp. At six foot five, he was hard to miss, and he could blast a baseball a long ways, but it was his mouth that earned him most of his notoriety. After a strikeout, he'd quote Shakespeare, grumbling, "What a foul and 'muddy-mettled' creature I am, peaked like a 'John-a-dream, unpregnant of my cause.'" If an opposing batter struck out, Connors would yell from his position at first base, "Oh, 'the whips and scorns of time!'" If the ump missed a call, Connors would admonish the arbiter with, "'The slings and arrows of outrageous fortune' I can take, but your blindness is ridiculous."

Much would fall into place for the Dodgers in 1949. Roy Campanella would become the regular catcher, Carl Furillo would have his first outstanding year (106 RBIS, .322 batting average), Duke Snider would go from five home runs and 21 RBIS in 1948 to 23 home runs and 92 RBIS, and Don Newcombe would join the team after the season started, ending the year with a staff-high of 17 victories.

The main focus in spring training was solving the problem at first base. And what a "muddy-mettled" situation it was. On April 3 the *Brooklyn Eagle* printed that a trade had brought the Dodgers New York Giant slugger Johnny Mize. When that trade unraveled, the name of Philly first baseman Dick Sisler came up. Also mentioned were Dodger farmhands Dee Fondy and Preston Ward. (Ward had batted .260 in 38 games at first base as a 22-year-old the previous year.)

And what about Gil Hodges? Hodges had played 96 games at first base in 1948, but he'd hit only .248 and was still thought of as a catcher—he had caught 38 games that year.

On April 8 the Dodgers brought in left-handed Chuck Connors for a trial, just as the team was to tour Georgia. At the time, Connors had gone 17 for 24 while playing for Clyde Sukeforth's squad in the minor league camp. The 28-year-old Connors was coming off a season in which he had batted .307 for the Montreal Royals, Brooklyn's top farm team.

"I've never been with a loser yet," said the brash and good-natured Connors when told of his promotion. "When do we start printing World Series tickets?"

Connors would soon be regaling his teammates with light verse, such as "The Shooting of Dan McGrew," "The Face on the Barroom Floor" ("I shot a man today, and I don't care"), and the old standard that Connors appropriated and made his own, "Casey at the Bat."

But the frivolity would have to wait. When Connors joined the Dodgers, the team was in Macon, Georgia, and the situation was serious. Whites and blacks had never played on the same ball field before in Georgia during a professional game, and the Ku Klux Klan attempted to organize a boycott of the game in Macon as well as of the following two contests planned for Atlanta.

As it turned out, no disruptions occurred other than the occasional boo, but there was tension and a feeling of uncertainty in the stands and on the field. The box score shows that Chuck Connors, in his first day in a Brooklyn Dodger uniform, played alongside Jackie Robinson for the historic game in Macon. Connors had also played alongside Robinson in Montreal in 1946—Robinson's first year in Organized Baseball. Judging from newspaper quotes by Connors in subsequent years, he was proud to be on the field when baseball finally made the transition to an integrated sport. He may have only played a supporting role in the drama, but Connors was a thinker and he knew which issues were the important ones.

◆ ◆ ◆

Chuck Connors's life, eventful and varied, began April 10, 1921. He was born to Allan and Marcella Connors, Irish immigrants who had lived for a while in Newfoundland before settling in—where else?—Brooklyn. And that's where Chuck Connors was born and raised. Connors would often remark that the events of his early years affected him profoundly. "Everything I am or am ever going to be was set in those first years, before I was 14," he once said.

The first critical event came during the Depression when, during a long illness, Allan Connors lost his job. The family then moved from a modest home in a working-class section of Brooklyn to a $30 a month flat in a run-down section of the borough. If they needed hot water, they had to boil it. Money was so scarce they couldn't even afford a radio. Connors recalled how, occasionally, if weather permitted, he would listen to a neighbor's radio through his open window. In the winter it was freezing cold in the apartment; there was no heat. In the summer there was no fan; the family suffered accordingly.

At the lowest point the family went on relief. For a year and a half they received $50 a month from the government—not much but enough to keep the family afloat. Marcella Connors got a job scrubbing floors in office buildings at night. Allan Connors apparently lost much of his enthusiasm for life and it wasn't until a few years later that he began working again, as a night watchman. Chuck Connors said later that the poverty he endured as a child was part of the reason he was so motivated later. His father may have lost his ambitions; but Chuck Connors became a scrapper.

Full of energy, Chuck (or Kevin, as he was also then known) was playing a ball game of his own invention against a wall in the neighborhood one day when John Flynn happened by. Flynn worked as a bank teller. Although married, he was childless, but he loved kids and organized a youth team called the Bay Ridge Celtics. He asked young Connors if he played baseball, and Connors nodded yes. Chuck Connors was then 13. For the next four years he was coached by John Flynn and immersed himself in all aspects of the Bay Ridge Boys Club. Connors always maintained that joining the club was the most important event in his life.

Brooklyn's Adelphi Academy also figures prominently in the Chuck Connors story. After making a name for himself in local athletics, Connors was admitted to the private high school on an athletic scholarship. He played baseball, basketball, and football. His high school yearbook reads, "Kevin . . . aspires to be a big league baseball player." He made it clear that his goal was to someday play first base for the Brooklyn Dodgers.

While at Adelphi, Connors developed his interest in Shakespeare and other verse. It was because of a girl named Mary Nolan. What they had might be called a crush, and it was expressed in poetry the two sent to each other.

Another pivotal event in his life occurred at Seton Hall University, which he selected after turning down a reported 27 other athletic scholarships. It seems Chuck was wisecracking in class, and a teacher, Father Gilhooley, chastised him: "If you like to talk so much, I suggest you enter the declamatory contest." The declamatory contest was a big event at Seton Hall. Connors chose to recite Vachel Lindsay's long and dramatic poem, "The Congo" ("Mumbo-Jumbo will hoo-doo you. Beware, beware, walk with care. Boomlay, boomlay, boomlay, Boom.") Connors's powerful voice, chiseled good looks, and strong personality kept the audience and judges transfixed; he was declared the winner. This was a major turning point for Connors. He had tasted the sweet elixir known to those who have pleased a crowd, and he was hooked.

Seton Hall was eye-opening for Connors in many ways. Years later he said, "I was invited to splendid homes that I never believed existed even in my wildest dreams. Classmates often came to school in chauffeur-driven limousines." Connors said that even though there was nothing fancy about him, including his wardrobe, he didn't feel rejected. He was motivated by what he saw. "I wanted to be part of that scene," he said.

The number-one sport at Seton Hall was basketball, and Connors played on a powerhouse team with future NBA great and pro basketball Hall of Famer Bob Davies. But baseball was Connors's real love, and when the Dodgers offered the first baseman a contract in 1940, he signed. (Another story is that the Dodgers arranged his scholarship at Seton Hall with the understanding Connors would later sign with Brooklyn.)

The first stop in pro baseball for Chuck Connors was Newport, Arkansas, a small town of about 5,000. Future major league standout Johnny Sain put in two good years with Newport in 1938 and 1939, learning much of his craft in the Class D Northwest Arkansas League, but Connors's first season was abbreviated and in all regards dismal. His trip from the East Coast to Arkansas resulted in appearances in only four games—he went one for eleven before breaking his finger in a loss to Paragould. That was the end of his season and he returned east. In the fall Connors once again attended classes at Seton Hall.

He apparently had mixed thoughts about what to do with his baseball career and went on the voluntary retired list for 1941. In 1942 famed Yankee scout Paul Kritchell, who had seen Connors play baseball in college, came across Connors's name on a list of unprotected players and, even though it was news to him that Connors had pro experience, drafted him. Connors, figuring the military would also soon be drafting him—and knowing that he might not come back from the service in one piece if at all—decided to take the Yankee offer.

Connors was sent to the Norfork, Virginia, team in late June of 1942 as a replacement for first baseman Joe Collins. Collins, who would later appear in seven World Series with the Yankees, was hitting only .133 and was sent to a lower classification where he got his game back on track. Connors did a credible job for Norfolk, batting .264 and driving in 45 runs in 72 games. Besides Collins and Connors, other eventual major leaguers on that team were pitchers Vic Raschi and Bill Wight.

Wight, a longtime player and scout, remembers Chuck Connors's batting style: "He had a big swing, and he had good leverage. If the pitcher got the ball out over the plate, he could drive the ball. He was a power hitter." Wight also mentioned that he didn't recall Connors doing any on-field clowning at that point in his career. "He was just a ballplayer at that time and trying to get higher."

In November of 1942 the draft board made the expected call. As always, Connors stood out—even in the Army. He was assigned to a tank unit in Camp Campbell, Kentucky, but before long he was sent to West Point, where he trained cadets in tank maintenance and operation. He was so well liked that he was allowed to play basketball on leave occasionally with the American Basketball League's Brooklyn Indians (with Bob Davies who was also on military leave).

Upon release from the Army in the spring of 1946, Connors was assigned to one of the Yankees' two Triple A farm teams, the Newark Bears. Connors later claimed that he had had a good spring but wanted to play for the Dodgers and had sent Branch Rickey Jr. daily letters asking the Dodger executive to arrange a trade. Whatever the true story behind the move may have been, the Dodgers picked up Connors from the Yankees on waivers on April 23, 1946, and assigned him to Montreal, where Jackie Robinson was just breaking in.

Connors played in a few spring training games with Montreal during that period and after three weeks was transferred to the Dodgers' team in Newport News, Virginia, in the Piedmont League.

The late 1940s were years Chuck Connors would remember fondly. In 1946 he played with a young catcher named Gil Hodges and had his first solid year in pro ball, hitting .293 with 17 home runs and a career high 19 stolen bases. At Mobile, Alabama, in 1947 the team won its first South Atlantic League championship since 1922, and Chuck and the other players earned a special place in the hearts of the local fans. (In 1987 the players were all enshrined as honorary inductees of the Mobile Sports Hall of Fame's inaugural group. Chuck Connors was there for the ceremonies, along with former teammates Stan Wasiak, Cal Abrams, Pat McGlothin, George Shuba, and others.)

Connors, a basketball center whose strength was on defense, played for the National Basketball League champion Rochester Royals in 1945–46. Bob Davies and Red Holtzman were two of the starters. Besides Connors, backups included football's Otto Graham and major league catcher Del Rice. Connors played basketball for the Boston Celtics in 1946–47, but years later he explained, "Once I came to Mobile and started to rise and become more successful, I quit basketball and concentrated just on baseball."

In 1948 the Dodgers moved Connors up to Montreal where he had a good year (17 home runs, 88 RBIs, .307 batting average) and was a teammate of Turk Lown, Don Newcombe, Duke Snider, and Clyde King. That was also the year Connors met Canadian model Elizabeth Jane Riddell on a blind date. The two were married four months later and had four sons together. They divorced in 1962.

In 1949 Connors achieved the goal he'd been striving for since boyhood. He played well enough in spring training to make it onto the roster of the Brooklyn Dodgers. Gil Hodges had a great spring (and would have an excellent season) and Connors's job was to back up Hodges at first base.

By May 1 the Dodgers had won six and lost six and were playing at home against the Phillies. The box score shows names like Reese, Campanella, Robinson, Cox, Hodges, Furillo, Ashburn, Hamner, Waitkus, and Ennis. Preacher Roe started the game for Brooklyn; Russ Meyer tossed for the Phils. Meyer went into the ninth with a 4–2 lead, and with one out Gil Hodges singled, bringing the potential tying run to the plate. The Dodgers would go on to win the pennant by only one game—every game counted. Over the PA it was announced, "Now batting for Furillo, Chuck Connors." It really was a "Casey at the Bat" situation. Although he couldn't win the game, Connors could tie it or at least keep the rally going. The table was set for the tall Irish kid who had grown up 10 blocks from

Ebbets Field. But in front of 20,507 spectators, the hometown kid failed in the clutch. It was his one and only plate appearance for the Brooklyn Dodgers in a major league game.

Chuck Connors joked about this one at bat for the rest of his life, but in reality it must have given him much pain. Connors hit a grounder back to Russ Meyer, who threw to Granny Hamner at second for the force on Hodges. Hamner, after a quick pivot, then threw to Waitkus at first, erasing Connors and ending the game.

Manager Burt Shotton was asked later why he had sent Connors up, and with a grimace he explained to a reporter from the *Brooklyn Eagle,* "To reduce the possibilities of a double play."

But that's life. We don't dislike Casey for striking out; it's just an unfortunate occurrence. And before we feel too bad for Chuck Connors, let's remember his marvelous life. And besides, most of us would give anything to have batted even once in a major league game. In a 1959 article Cecil Smith of the *L.A. Times* wrote about attending a game with Chuck Connors, who at the time was at the height of his show business success:

> They all know Chuck from his first base days, including the large, gentlemanly Gil Hodges who kept Chuck out of the majors. "But for Gil," I said, "you might be playing for the Dodgers. . . ."
> "Ssssh!" said Chuck. "He'd be the Rifleman!"

Connors was bringing in a reported $150,000 a year at that point, more than Ted Williams, Mickey Mantle, or any other ballplayer. Within 10 years he'd be one of the most well-paid entertainers in the world, earning an estimated $20,000 a week.

◆ ◆ ◆

Twelve days after pinch hitting for Carl Furillo in his one and only at bat for the Brooklyn Dodgers, Chuck Connors was sent back to Montreal (Don Newcombe went from Montreal to the Dodgers), and Connors had two more fine years with the Royals. In 1949 he hit .319 with 108 RBIS, and in 1950 he batted .290. The irrepressible Connors was popular in Montreal, but because he was so outgoing fans in some cities would heckle him nonstop. Connors recalled for Sid

Ziff of the *L.A. Times* how he responded once to the fans in Rochester. "I brought 16 pounds of raw hamburger in a package to the park with me and put it on the bench. The first time they started on me, I brought out the hamburger and began throwing it by the handful to the crowd. With each handful I'd yell, 'Eat, you wolves! *Eat!*' The fans were so astounded they actually did eat the hamburger."

After the 1950 season Brooklyn traded Connors along with another minor league first baseman, Dee Fondy, to the Chicago Cubs for outfielder Hank Edwards and cash. The Cubs were looking for an eventual replacement for their popular first baseman, Phil Cavarretta, who wasn't over the hill yet but was slowing down. Fondy was kept with the parent club when the season started in 1951; Connors was told he might be brought up later in the season and was optioned to the Cubs' top minor league team, the Los Angeles Angels.

In early June Connors was tearing up the Coast League, hitting .321 with 22 home runs in 98 games, when Chicago beckoned. He was given a real opportunity to show what he could do on the major league level. Unfortunately, Connors, who ended his career with a lifetime batting average of .300 at the Triple A level, probably didn't quite have the ability to succeed in the bigs—but at least he got the chance; many players didn't.

Chuck Connors was a proficient fielder, nimble, agile, and with his height and reach he presented a big target for the other infielders. He swung with an uppercut, which is fine for a batter with a great eye who hits the ball on the button, with power, a high percentage of the time. But Connors, at six foot five, had a huge strike zone and a swing like his left him vulnerable to major league pitchers who could throw a ball with pinpoint accuracy to a spot in the strike zone, high and inside, where Connors couldn't handle it.

He was given a chance by the Cubs, and he had to be grateful for that. And he got off on the right foot. In Connors's first game he went two for three, and then he went two for four the next day. He started most of the Cubs games the rest of the season but tapered off and ended at .239. (One more hit and it would have been .244, which certainly looks a lot better than .239. A few leg hits wouldn't have hurt his cause.)

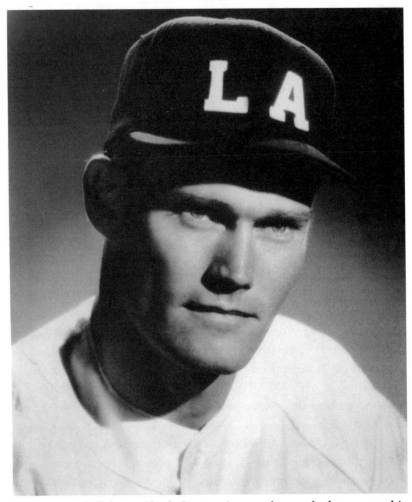

Movie star or ballplayer? Chuck Connors in 1952, the year he last appeared in baseball, and one year after he had begun working his way into films as a bit player. (*Courtesy of Steven Stevens Sr.*)

In 1951 the Cubs finished last, and in July manager Frankie Frisch was replaced by Phil Cavarretta. Dee Fondy hit .271 to Connors's .239, and became the Cubs' regular first baseman in 1952, hitting a combined .298 over the next three seasons. And Dee Fondy, almost four years younger than Connors, could motor; while in the Dodger chain he twice led his league in stolen bases. It's interesting to note, though, that the top hitting Cub first baseman in 1951 was the old man, Phil Cavarretta, who had 64 hits in

206 at bats for an average of .311. It's also interesting to note that the first of Chuck Connors's two home runs that year beat the New York Giants—one more win and the Giants would have finished the 1951 season ahead of Brooklyn, and there would have been no Dodgers-Giants playoff.

I called Phil Cavarretta to ask him about Chuck Connors. The Cubs' legendary first baseman said this about him:

> He was a wonderful guy the short time he was with the Cubs. He had a good sense of humor, no doubt about it. On some of our bus trips going to the airport he would recite poems. "Casey at the Bat." At that he was great. . . . He was a great guy on a ball club, and I loved him for that, because we had bad days and good days, and he kind of kept our spirits up.
>
> He didn't play that much because I had Dee Fondy there, and I was a part-time player. Dee Fondy was a good ballplayer and I was trying to do some things with him. Not that I neglected Chuck. I had two young men there, and I tried to pick the best one. When you're the manager, you try, along with your coaches, you try to select your best players. And we could see Dee Fondy, as he went on to prove, he was a good ballplayer. He could run like a deer, and actually Chuck, as far as his speed was concerned, he wasn't what you would call a gazelle. As a man, as a person, I loved him. If I had to have him as a son, I would have loved to had him as a son. That's how much I thought of the guy.
>
> We farmed him out to Los Angeles, our Triple A club. Unfortunately his ability didn't call for a recall. But, possibly, in his life it was the best thing that ever happened to him. Because he went out to the coast there, among the Hollywood stars, and this is the way he became a TV and movie star.

Chuck Connors had been popular in Montreal and other minor league stops such as Mobile, Alabama, and Newport News, Virginia, but in Los Angeles not only was he popular—very popular— but he was also appreciated. The show business people understood his abilities and saw his potential.

(Left) Teenage Chuck Connors working out at Brooklyn's Ebbets Field during the late 1930s. (Right) The Chicago Cubs' Chuck Connors in 1951. (*Courtesy of Steven Stevens Sr.*)

Besides his excellent half-season playing with Los Angeles in 1951, Connors also played with the team in 1952—his last season in pro ball. He injured both shoulders in 1952 and managed to hit only .259, but while playing for Los Angeles, Connors was at his extroverted best. He was known to forgo the customary home run trot in favor of improvised routines. Some claim that on occasion he slid into every base after knocking the ball over the fence, and at least once, according to Connors himself, he slid into second, cartwheeled to third, and crawled home. Another version is that he leaped around the bases like a lunatic and then finished with a flourish, sliding home on his belly.

Connors made many friends in the entertainment business. "Many movie people are baseball fans," Connors once told reporter Hedda Hopper, "and that's how I got into pictures. Billy Grady of Metro called me one day to say he had a bit part in a picture he thought I could do." That was in 1951. Wrote Hopper, "Chuck got five hundred dollars for his three days' work, asked how long this had been going on, and promptly asked for another part." Connors added, "Grady said he didn't have anything so I suggested he call one of his friends." This led to a small part at 20th Century Fox, and then Connors returned to Grady for more work.

Connors's first role was that of a puzzled police captain in *Pat and Mike* who tried to get to the bottom of a situation involving Katharine Hepburn and Spencer Tracy. Other early movies included *South Sea Woman, Code Two,* and *Trouble Along the Way.*

Reporters (and Connors) over the years presented Connors as someone who pretty much stumbled into a career in movies and television, but most likely he prepared for many years. Bill Wight, his teammate at Norfolk in 1942, also lived at a boardinghouse with Connors that year. Said Wight, "Apparently he had some voice training because he sounded pretty professional, even then. Once in a while he'd run a little poetry at you, a little Shakespeare. I think he had ambitions to get into the stage or the movies because he trained for it. He prepared himself. He didn't just flounder into this thing. Dedicated guy. Very nice fellow, by the way." Wight added that he enjoyed hearing Connors's recitations of "Casey at the Bat" and also the Shakespearean verse. "I was very impressed with that," said Wight. "I never heard anybody do it before. He had a good delivery, good voice. He probably practiced delivery and stuff in his room. I wouldn't be surprised."

A few months after the 1952 season (Connors hadn't announced his retirement from baseball yet) Jeane Hoffman wrote a delightful piece on him for the *L.A. Times:*

Mr. Kevin Joseph Aloysious Connors, who holds the PCL, AAU and RBI record for reciting "Casey at the Bat" 97,853 times (not counting two Rotary luncheons when he lost his voice) is now an actor. There seems to be some doubt that he was ever anything but. Anyhow, now that he's completed his sixth movie role this winter, the talented Connors is entitled to call himself a purified, Swift-premium gold-sealed ham.

"But I want to get one thing straight," added Connors. "Baseball comes first. Everything I've had in acting has come through baseball." Thirty-two-year-old Connors pounded the table as two termites ducked for cover. "If any theatrical parts interfere with my playing first base for the Angels, I'll turn 'em down. I'll admit I'm working toward a full-time acting career eventually."

Connors's agent at the time was George Goodale, who met him while working as the publicist for the Angels. Jeane Hoffman ended her story on Connors with,

"We are just thankful," sighed Goodale wearily, "that he has found something else to do than recite 'Casey at the Bat.'"

In early February of 1953 Chuck Connors announced his retirement from baseball. Here's an excerpt from his letter to Angel President Don Stewart:

In terms of family and future I feel I have taken the proper step. Five years of professional basketball have shortened my playing years in baseball. In all honesty I don't believe there are more than two high-quality seasons left in me. I have no guarantee that my shoulders, injured last year, have completely healed. My career in baseball has reached the twilight stage.

Some movie roles came Connors's way the next few years, but success didn't come overnight. He sold insurance, did a Pacific Coast League pregame show on local TV, and for a while sold water softener door-to-door. Connors and his wife had three small boys, and a fourth would arrive before the decade was over.

After forgotten low-budget movies such as *Naked Alibi, Target Zero, Hot Rod Girl,* and *Walk the Dark Street* (in addition to numerous television appearances), Connors landed a role in Walt Disney's 1957 release, *Old*

Yeller. He was cast as the understanding, compassionate father. Because he was so convincing, he was offered the role of the understanding, compassionate father, Lucas McCain, in *The Rifleman*—the show that would bring him to national prominence.

Connors, a driven and ambitious (and well-liked) man, was also nobody's fool. Even though it was a great part, he held out for 10 percent of the show's profits in addition to his salary. Said Connors, "I'd read how unhappy Hugh O'Brian *[Wyatt Earp]* and Clint Walker *[Cheyenne]* were, so when I signed the contract I felt if it was going to tie me down I wanted it to be worthwhile financially."

Connors worked at his craft with a vengeance. Early on he figured out that a cowboy wouldn't be believable speaking with a Brooklyn accent. Years later he told reporter Rick DuBrow how he prepared for his big break: "After two years in pictures, I had never been in a western, and my secret desire was to be a Gary Cooper. I was tall, thin and looked like one of those guys. But I also had a Brooklyn accent, didn't know how to ride a horse and wore a crew cut that hardly looked western." Then Connors bought a horse. "It had a game leg," he said. "The wrangler wouldn't sell me a real good one. Anyway, I rented an acre of land, fenced it and started learning on my own. I fed the horse, watered it—prepared for what I wanted. I worked on the accent and let the hair grow."

Throughout his career Connors downplayed his acting ability, but he in fact shined in many roles—and not just in westerns. The president of Four Star Pictures, Tom McDermott, once told *Look Magazine*, "Chuck will be around a long time. He won't be a star who goes through the roof, then drops. He could end up a hell of a star." Added Jean Eaton, also of Four Star, "This guy is a real leader. There's nothing he's not interested in. And if he wants to know, he goes to an expert. . . . He's not just one of these ham actors."

Many of those close to Chuck Connors mentioned his intelligence. His secretary, Rose Mary Grumley, once told a reporter that each year Connors would read 250 books. "And so help me," she said, "he retains it all. He's amazing!"

Personable, intelligent, athletic, handsome, and articulate, Connors had his faults, and he was the first to admit it. When interviewed by Melvin Durslag in the mid-sixties, he talked candidly about many things but made a request of the writer: "Knock me, but leave me a future." Connors explained to Durslag,

> After I got started in *The Rifleman* I got a big head. I felt the world was made for me. I was one of those poor, sick, sorry guys who gained something known as "stardom," and I thought I was something special. I didn't realize at the time that I was nothing more than a ballplayer who got lucky.
>
> They told me I had to attend this function and that one and stay in the spotlight and build up my image. So I did what they said. I was soon attending the right premieres, appearing on the right shows, being seen in the right places, eating rich foods and staying up late. And, in return, I was being bored to death and traveling in circles I despised. One by one I started eliminating things I didn't like. The first thing that went were those phony cocktail parties.

Connors told another writer in 1966,

> If it weren't for baseball and golf I'd go mad in Hollywood. Maybe baseball is a healthier, purer way of making a living. . . . I'm more comfortable with sports people. I'm not from the same cloth as show people, although I like and respect many of them. Actually, I feel I'm stealing money in their business.

In the late sixties some newspapers ran stories discussing the possibility of Chuck Connors running for political office, and not just any office—the actor was contemplating running for the U.S. Senate. Connors, a resident of southern California since he moved from Brooklyn in the summer of 1951, had befriended Ronald Reagan, Richard Nixon, and other conservative politicians and admitted that he indeed was thinking about running for office. But Connors was probably too outspoken to be a successful politician. In an article in February of 1968 in the *L.A. Times,* Connors told writer Turnley Walker about his connection with politics:

> Toward the end of Reagan's campaign for governor, I wanted to help him. I believed in him as a person, a qualified man, and I believed the state needed a drastic change of government. So I said, what can I do? What I did was make a five-minute spot,

in my own words. I wrote it. It played on TV all over the state. I liked the big reaction it got.

Then the day before the election I made about 20 campaign appearances. Shopping centers, community gathering places, big crowds. I got a thrill out of the way the crowds greeted me. Can't deny it. Felt great. There I was talking politics, and they were hanging on every word. Cheering. Their eyes and faces, they really liked me. And I thought, hell, I can do this! Nothing to it! These people already know who I am, and they're so damned ready for someone! Anyone!

But Connors decided not to seek office. He explained,

I'll stay with my own convictions. They've been developing all my life. If I ran for office, I'd have to go with the conservative leaders, and I'm not right for them. I believe in welfare. In relief. I only want to make it sounder, more effective. I think they want to destroy it. I believe in the value of the intellectuals. They don't. For me morality is not tied up in some church orthodoxy. For them it is.

Even though he was labeled a conservative (self-labeled a "fiscal conservative"), it was clear Connors analyzed issues on an individual basis. "The damned liberal and conservative points of views are so polarized. You can't get at the truth that way," he said. In 1983 he further explained why he had never run for office: "Being around so many politicians, I became a little cynical about politicians in general."

Connors probably felt that if he'd been elected to the Senate or some other post, he would have eventually ruffled the feathers of the electorate. Connors wasn't a mainstream guy; sooner or later he would have proved too outrageous for the general public.

This story illustrates the point. In the late 1960s Connors was invited into the television booth during a nationally broadcast baseball game. An up-and-coming young star lined a ball into the gap and turned what looked like a double into a three-base hit. The announcer exclaimed, "Looks like the young fellow is quite a hitter." Added Connors, "Yeah, the f****r can run too!"

By the time he died in November of 1992, Connors had appeared in more than 60 movies—including *The Big Country; Geronimo; Move*

Over, Darling; Flipper; Support Your Local Gunfighter; Soylent Green; and *Airplane II: The Sequel*—and countless television shows. He was nominated for an Emmy for his performance in *Roots* and played the lead in seven television series, including *Branded, Cowboy in Africa,* and *The Thrill Seekers* as well as *The Rifleman.* In 1983 he told a writer that he didn't mind being remembered primarily for *The Rifleman:*

> It's no problem at all for me. My whole ability to make a living is derived from the fact that I was *The Rifleman.* My life is pretty good now. I've had my bumps along the way, personally. But I've got a tremendous relationship with my four sons, have four or five very good friends and a lot of nice acquaintances. I have a nice ranch, pretty good health, and I don't ever have to work again.

Early in his acting career, in 1954, Connors told an interviewer, "I'm no great actor. I'm just lucky, but I think I'll make it in Hollywood." The writer added, "He will. You'll hear and see a lot of him. Whenever he feels his hat getting tight he reminds himself of his credo: 'Talent is God-given. Be humble. Fame is man-given. Be grateful. Conceit is self-given. Be careful.'"

People often use the word *luck* when talking about Chuck Connors. He used the word himself. He was lucky, true, but also talented. And he worked his butt off to achieve what he did.

Athletic throughout his life—he swam and ran to stay in shape—Connors also kept fit by mending fences, clearing brush, and operating a tractor on the high desert ranch near Tehachapi in southern California where he lived in his later years. He was at his ranch when a reporter from the *Mobile Press Register* called in 1986 to ask him to reflect on his past. Connors said, "I did have a goal in life. It was to play with the Brooklyn Dodgers and it came true. I've been a very fortunate man."

Kevin Joseph Aloysius (Chuck) Connors

Born April 10, 1921, Brooklyn, NY. Died November 10, 1992, Los Angeles, CA.
Batted left, threw left. Height: 6' 5½". Weight: 212 lbs.

Year	Club	League	G	AB	R	H	2B	3B	HR	RBI	SB	BA
1940	Newport	Northeast Arkansas	4	11	1	1	0	0	0	1	0	.091
1941	Johnstown	Pennsylvania State Association				(voluntarily retired)						
1942	Norfolk	Piedmont	72	250	28	66	9	6	5	45	2	.264
1943–45						(in United States Army)						
1946	Newport News	Piedmont	119	430	72	126	29	6	17	68	19	.293
1947	Mobile	Southern Association	145	514	65	131	29	6	15	82	10	.255
1948	Montreal	International	147	512	79	157	36	5	17	88	9	.307
1949	Montreal	International	133	477	90	152	25	5	20	108	6	.319
1949	Brooklyn	National	1	1	0	0	0	0	0	0	0	.000
1950	Montreal	International	121	407	69	118	26	4	6	68	14	.290
1951	Los Angeles	Pacific Coast	98	390	75	125	28	2	22	77	8	.321
1951	Chicago	National	66	201	16	48	5	1	2	18	4	.239
1952	Los Angeles	Pacific Coast	113	406	50	105	27	2	6	51	4	.259
		Major League totals	67	202	16	48	5	1	2	18	4	.238
		Minor League totals	952	3397	529	981	209	36	108	588	72	.289

3

THE BEST THE HALL LEFT OUT

BILL LANGE

Walter Langford toured the country about 10 years ago and interviewed stars from the 1920s, '30s, and '40s. I read the book of interviews he published (Legends of Baseball, Diamond Communications, 1987) and liked it. I wrote Langford and told him I wanted him to contribute a chapter to my book. We talked on the phone a few times and sent a few letters back and forth, but his wife was recovering from an injury and Langford decided he'd better decline. However, he suggested I contact his friend Bob Broeg, longtime Sporting News columnist and author of several books. Broeg wrote the definitive book on Stan Musial as well as the classic Superstars of Baseball. I knew his reputation as one of the most respected writers in baseball—he's on the Veterans Committee of the Hall of Fame and is also the only writer on the Hall's board of directors—and I knew I'd love to have him write a chapter for this collection; his perspective would be most welcome.

I wrote him and then we talked on the phone. What a nice man. I can see why he's so well-liked. But he kept turning me down. I kept pestering him and finally he gave in. His note to me said, "You win." He commended me for my perseverance, which he said he hoped would pay off for me in the long run. (This was before I had a book contract.)

The player I wanted Broeg to profile was Bill Lange. I had noticed Lange for the first time about six months earlier while thumbing through the Baseball

Encyclopedia. *Lange had a lifetime batting average of .330 and I knew nothing about him. I did some research on him at the San Francisco Public Library and found him to be an exceptional star, an amazing talent who was a favorite of sportswriters and adored by the fans.*

Here's Bob Broeg's profile of Bill Lange.

> After seeing them all come and go for nearly 30 years; after seeing the great ones and the little ones, those who starred for years, and those who passed early from the game, two figures of them all persist in forcing themselves upon my memory, and in plain opposition to each other—the forms of Tyrus Cobb and William Lange. Somehow, someway, these two always present themselves before me for comparison, and despite all the praise they lavish on the Georgian today, I cannot see where the gigantic Lange was his inferior.
>
> —W. A. (Bill) Phelon
> *Baseball Magazine*, 1915

If Dan Cupid hadn't thrown a curved arrow at him, Bill Lange would be remembered now for what he obviously was, one of the best ballplayers ever.

But Lange, the fun-loving genial giant nicknamed "Little Eva"— of all things—left baseball early to marry and take a doting father-in-law's job offer back home in San Francisco.

There's a 10-year minimum for Hall of Fame consideration, so Lange, "The Player Who Quit Too Soon," doesn't qualify. Otherwise there no doubt would be a plaque with his name hanging on a wall at Cooperstown.

Clark Griffith and Connie Mack, two of the game's most knowledgeable observers, had plenty of praise for our forgotten hero, Mr. Lange.

Of the seven-season veteran, not yet 30 when Cupid curved him, longtime Washington club owner Griffith hailed his former teammate as "the best outfielder I ever saw." He added, "I've seen all the great ones—Tris Speaker, Ty Cobb, Joe DiMaggio, and others—but I consider Bill Lange the equal of, if not better than, all other outfielders."

Griffith's analysis was part of a 1945 piece in *Collier's* magazine by Talbert Josselyn. The title was a heady tribute: "Better Than the

Best." Accompanying it was a grinning photo of a round-faced fella, close to 75, looking much younger and robust, displaying the cheerful, outgoing disposition that obviously was part of his trademark.

As Griffith put it,

> Aside from Bill's great capabilities hitting, fielding, throwing, and running, he had a remarkable disposition. He was always in good humor, always had a smile on his face, even when he was sliding and knocking down men who were trying to tag him at a base. He was the toughest, roughest base runner who ever strode the bases, but no one ever got mad at him.
>
> He had a seventh sense as a base runner in timing throws. In other words, he used to watch the ball and arrive at the bag just ahead of the throw so that he could knock the baseman down, making him lose the ball altogether.

Obviously, Lange's six-foot-two, 200-pound-plus physique gave him an intimidating and actual edge, and the rampant way he ran for the Chicago Nationals from 1893 through 1899 certainly must have caused the rule makers to take a sharper look at the regulations.

Griffith told of a play that began routinely enough when Lange hit a slow roller to shortstop. Lange was going to beat it out, but he slowed up just a bit, timing his arrival so that he could upend the first baseman an instant before the ball got there. Then Lange headed for second and bowled over the fielder as the ball came in. The ball went into left field, and Lange galloped toward third, where he repeated the routine and headed for the plate. The ball got there first, the catcher steadied himself, but Lange was too much for him. He dropped the ball, and Lange scored. As Griffith put it, "He made a home run on a slow roller to shortstop."

Lange described his approach to base running in the 1945 *Collier's* article:

> I got on base any way I could. Then I took a big lead. If the pitcher threw to first, I went on to second. As I came in, I watched the eyes of the man taking the throw. If he was looking to the right, I threw my body to the right and took the ball on my shoulder. If he was looking to the left, I threw myself to

the left. If the ball bounced and rolled a few feet, I went on to third.

If the pitcher didn't throw to first, I waited until I was ready and stole on him. Sometimes I pulled the delayed steal—waited until the catcher tossed the ball back to the pitcher. I always tried to keep them guessing; tried to throw them off balance.

In 1895 a sportswriter wrote, "Lange encourages more profanity and poor throwing than any man in baseball. For it is the apparent desperation of his steals that causes the 'rattles' to seize the other team all at once."

Amos Rusie, who won 20 or more games eight seasons in a row and then didn't win another ball game, explained that it was Lange, inadvertently, who ended his career. Rusie worked on a quick, snap throw to try to pick Lange off first base. Rusie only tried it once, and the only thing that snapped was Rusie's arm.

Connie Mack, who was a young man himself once—a catcher during old Lange's time—called Lange's base running "the greatest I ever saw," which is saying something given that Connie had a great affection also for the fearless, reckless base running of Ty Cobb.

But if Lange reminded some of Tyrus the Terrible, it was only on the playing field, not off it. Big Bill was as happy as his Little Eva nickname, gained because his graceful, nimble moves on the field reminded a sportswriter of a famous dancer of the Naughty Nineties.

He was also gay in the traditional sense of the word, a gregarious mixer, a good storyteller, and always jovial. For example, when well into his seventies, he would answer his phone with, "This is a young fellow named Bill Lange speaking."

◆ ◆ ◆

William Alexander Lange, born in San Francisco in 1871, grew up in the sandlots of The Presidio, where his father was an Army sergeant of ordnance. Bill—or Billy as he was then known—played a little semipro ball in Port Townsend, Washington, and then made his debut in professional ball in 1891 as a catcher with Seattle. The minor league trail was a short one for Lange, ending in 1892 with Oakland.

Bill Lange, Chicago's "Prince of Thieves," ran the bases "like an intelligent buffalo." A superb outfielder with a powerful arm, he could also hit, once supposedly walloping a ball so hard that it sailed over the center field fence in Cincinnati and smashed through the window of a beer garden, breaking up a pinochle game. *(Courtesy of Transcendental Graphics)*

Before the 1893 season, he was acquired by the Chicago Colts, the National League antecedents of the Cubs, who were then managed by legendary Adrian Anson—"Cap" if you knew him early, "Pop" if the 22-year legend was on the shady side of his 3,000-hit career.

Lange didn't need much introduction to National League pitching. Fact is, except for hitting .281 in his rookie year, he hit with a consistency seldom seen—.328, .389, .326, .340, .319, and .325. His home runs, in an era when the ball wasn't much more than a beanbag, ranged up to 10, with an average of about 6. Three times he had more than 90 RBIs, although playing no more than 123 games. He had 84 stolen bases one season and a league-leading 73 when he played only 118 games in 1897.

Lange, a right-handed hitter, batted with power to the opposite field, leading to one of the best stories about the quick-thinking Toast of the Coast. Anticipating an intentional walk—there were runners on second and third and first base was open—Bill "sold" the umpire on the fact that if he switched sides in the batter's box before the pitcher released the ball, it was legal.

The pitcher went into his stretch, checked the runners, and Lange leaped across the plate, landing in the opposite batter's box. His back was to the plate as he spanked a wide pitch into right field for a two-run double. There was much arguing, of course, but the play was allowed.

Another time, Lange and Jimmy Ryan, another Chicago outfielder of note, contrived to pull off an equally outlandish maneuver. It was late in the game, top of the last inning. Chicago led by a run and was in the field. Two were out and one man was on base. Did I mention it was getting dark? It was getting quite dark, and the batter got ahold of one. It went over left fielder Ryan's head—a home run. But Ryan ran back and jumped and acted as if he had caught the ball. Lange got into the act and called for Ryan to throw him the imaginary ball. Ryan made the phantom toss, and Lange finished off the pantomime by catching the ball, putting it in his pocket, and jogging off the field. The wool was pulled over the squinting eyes of the umpire, players, and spectators; Chicago was credited with a victory.

THE BALL AFTER
LANGE'S SMASH.

Lange pointed out that he and Ryan weren't the only smart players back then. "The parks were full of them."

He told of a time a catcher had him believing he could score easily, that there would be no play at the plate. The catcher went into his act, threw his mask—and his glove—in the dirt, and Lange slowed up. Then the catcher "snatched the throw out of the air with his bare hand—it had been coming all the time—and slammed it into my ribs."

Among those Lange impressed most was another former catcher, a man Lange discovered playing amateur ball in California: Frank "Husk" Chance, whose name still stands rhythmic in the punchline of Franklin P. Adams's famous poem. Chance, the Peerless Leader of the great Cub teams of the early 1900s, said, "No one matched Bill Lange. He could field like Tris Speaker, run the bases as good as Ty Cobb, and only once did he fail to hit .300."

Honus Wagner told about the first time he tried to put a tag on Lange. The throw had him beat, but "He pulled the prettiest hook slide you ever saw, and there I was, standing sort of foolishlike, with the ball, and I was nowhere near him."

LANGE'S SLIDE HOME.

By 1896, Little Eva was the dimpled darling of Chicago baseball fans, outpolling his nearest competitor by six to one in a popularity contest. He had the management of the Chicago team wrapped around his little finger as well.

Just before spring training was to begin in 1897, Lange let it be known that he wanted a $500 raise, or he wouldn't report. Without delay, Chicago management granted the raise. But Lange wasn't happy about it, not completely. He wanted to see the heavyweight championship fight between James J. Corbett and Bob Fitzsimmons in Carson City, Nevada, in March. That's why he had asked for a raise. The raise was a ruse to stall for time.

Never at a loss, Lange talked to a writer friend and persuaded him to plant a story saying Lange had been injured. The Chicago officials were quite concerned, but Lange wired back that the injury was not severe. He reported to spring training after he had healed which, remarkably, was just a short while after the boxing match.

After the 1899 season, at the height of his popularity and when only 28 years old, Bill Lange announced his retirement.

Wrote Lange at the time, "Plant flowers on my baseball grave out in center field, for I am in love and will never play there again."

When the team began to realize he was serious, they offered him some serious salary increases. It was reported they offered him two times—even three times—what he had been getting.

"BILL" LANGE SAYS ADIEU TO HIS CHICAGO ADMIRERS.

But Lange wanted to stay in California. His bride wanted him to stay, and his new father-in-law offered to help him get started in a career in real estate.

When the 1900 baseball season got under way, it was Danny Green in center field for the Chicago team; Bill Lange's baseball career was over.

Lange remained as popular in San Francisco as he had been in Chicago. He and his wife were the darlings of the social set. The women were charmed by Lange's fancy moves on the dance floor, and he entertained one and all with his tales of the diamond.

Business boomed. He managed trusts and various properties. Was there a downside? The marriage ended, but Lange remarried. Life went on, merrily.

The Chicago fans kept a special place in their hearts for the star who quit too soon, and they sent him a special gift in 1912—a Chalmers car. They say Bill Lange cut quite a figure driving around San Francisco, nattily dressed, in his sparkling new automobile.

Lange's second marriage wasn't the ticket, and he tried matrimony once again. This time, Big Bill got "the treatment" from his friends.

Bill Lange, circa 1940 (*Courtesy of William A. Lange Jr.*)

Trying to slip quietly out of town for a simple wedding in Reno, Lange and his bride-to-be were "ambushed" in downtown San Francisco by a throng of friends, including several newspaper people. The next day, September 13, 1924, a story appeared in the *San Francisco Examiner* with the headline, "Bill Lange Again 'Slides' to the Altar," and the subhead, "Former Baseball Idol Leaves for Reno to Take Fair Telephone Girl as Third Bride." The article read, "Lange's friends are aggrieved. They wish him happiness, and all that, but they think he really ought to invite them to one of his weddings sometime."

But it's Bill Lange's baseball career that matters to us most, and we've saved one of his best stories for last.

Fined $100 for missing a Boston-to-New York train—when $100 wasn't salted peanuts—Lange overslept again two days later, missing the train to Washington.

Arriving late, he changed into his uniform in a cab and raced directly onto the field in the home half of the second inning. An extremely agitated Cap Anson let Lange know that there would be another hefty fine.

The game was tense into the eleventh when Chicago scored, but in the home half, with two out and the tying run on base, powerful-hitting Kip Selbach belted a long drive over Lange's head. Big Bill turned his back, raced hard to the fence, and just as he reached the barrier, he leaped, threw up his hands, and made a somersaulting catch, crashing so hard into the wood that he knocked a plank out of the fence.

Crafty Hugh Fullerton, the second writer ever given Hall of Fame recognition for his baseball perspicacity, called the catch the greatest he ever saw. It's no wonder a sportswriter once described Lange's hands thusly: "They hold on to everything they reach, and they reach everything."

And what about the fines? Naturally, Anson wiped them out. That's what Lange thought would happen, anyway. But when he asked Cap about it, he let him know that the fines had to be paid.

Years later, Cap Anson visited California and, while at a baseball game, told the reporters sitting with him what a tremendous ballplayer Bill Lange had been. When an outfielder misplayed a fly ball, letting it go over his head, Anson added, "Bill Lange could have caught that ball with his feet."

Bill Lange, larger than life, the subject of some of the craziest baseball stories ever told—many of which actually might be true—lived a long, full life and died in his native San Francisco in 1950 at the age of 79. Which stories are true and which ones exaggerations? We'll probably never know for sure. But this is certain: Lange was one of baseball's greatest personalities and a player whose ability was surpassed by very few. He may well be the greatest ballplayer never inducted into the Hall of Fame.

William (Bill) Alexander Lange

Born June 6, 1871, San Francisco, CA. Died July 23, 1950, San Francisco, CA.
Batted right, threw right. Height: 6' 2". Weight: 200 lbs.

Year	Club	League	Position	G	AB	R	H	2B	3B	HR	RBI	SB	BA
1890	Port Townsend		C	(independent league—no record available)									
1891	Port Townsend		C	(independent league—no record available)									
1891	Seattle	Pacific NW	C-P	35	126	15	36					13	.286
1892	Seattle	Pacific NW	C	55	214	53	65					37	.304
1892	Oakland	California	C-OF	51	198	41	57					27	.288
1893	Chicago	National	2-O-3-S-C	117	469	92	132	8	7	8	88	47	.281
1894	Chicago	National	OF-SS-3B	111	442	84	145	16	9	6	90	65	.328
1895	Chicago	National	OF	123	478	120	186	27	16	10	98	67	.389
1896	Chicago	National	OF-C	122	469	114	153	21	16	4	92	84	.326
1897	Chicago	National	OF	118	479	119	163	24	14	5	83	73*	.340
1898	Chicago	National	OF-1B	113	442	79	141	16	10	6	69	22	.319
1899	Chicago	National	OF-1B	107	416	81	135	21	7	1	58	41	.325
	Major League totals—7 years			811	3195	689	1055	133	79	40	578	399	.330

Pitching Record

Year	Club	League	G	IP	W	L	PCT.	H	R	SO	BB
1891	Seattle	Pacific NW	11	76	4	3	.571	80	48	27	29

*Led league

4

A PLAYER FOR THE WORLD

DAVE ROBERTS

Back in the mid-1960s, when I was in my early teens, I collected baseball cards, some of which I still have. One of the cards I saved was a 1963 rookie card of longtime major leaguer Tommy Harper. Until recently, the three other players depicted on the card, Bob Saverine, Rogelio Alvarez, and Dave Roberts, were of no interest to me. Nearly thirty years after I acquired the card, I checked the records of the three nonstars and was intrigued by the fact that Dave Roberts had played nearly 1,500 minor league games. "Who is Dave Roberts," I wondered, "and why does he look so angry?" I began researching his career and that's how this book got started.

A left-handed batting and throwing outfielder and first baseman from Panama, Roberts began his baseball travels in 1952.

Like many minor leagues, the Southwest International League struggled to stay afloat. It only lasted two years. In 1951 members of the Tijuana team went on strike after repeatedly not being paid. In 1952, the last year of the league's existence, officials decided an all-black team would bring out the fans and increase revenues. The franchise, one of the most unusual in baseball history, started the preseason as the Riverside-Ensenada Comets, with home games scheduled for the United States and Mexico. Later that year the team moved to Porterville, California. That was Dave Roberts's first pro team.

Roberts was a high school junior in Panama when offered a contract by the Comets, and he had no idea what to expect. He had grown up reading *The Sporting News* and baseball books such as Joe DiMaggio's *Lucky to Be a Yankee* and was overwhelmed by what he found when he reached America. He recalls playing in Las Vegas and sleeping at the YMCA on smelly gym mats. Says Roberts, "I couldn't believe I was playing pro ball, from what I had read. The conditions, the discrimination, it just blew me away."

However, things turned out fairly well. The Porterville manager was Chet Brewer, the legendary Negro League pitcher. Brewer took the youngster under his wing. "Chet became like a second father to me," says Roberts. "He really took care of me. I think had it been anyone else, I probably would have jumped ship. Chet said, 'You stay here. You're gonna be a good ballplayer. You're gonna be fine.'"

Roberts was exclusively an outfielder in those days (he'd later learn to play first base), and in the field he was fast and had a strong arm. Because he didn't weigh much and was speedy, and because he peppered the field with line drives, Roberts was used early on as a leadoff batter. But his power couldn't be denied, and soon he was used in the number three and four spots, which is where he would bat most of his career.

Besides Chet Brewer, who pitched occasionally even at age 45, other Porterville teammates included ancient Andy Porter; Walt Tyler, a pitcher who hurt his arm and then led the league in hitting after being converted to the outfield by another team; and first baseman Tom Alston, who showed up during training camp uninvited and became the club's top hitter (as well as the St. Louis Cardinals' first black player two years later).

After the season, Roberts returned home to Panama, finished high school, and played the first of many seasons of winter ball. He felt good about his baseball prospects. "I felt that I was going to be all right. I felt good about where I was going."

Where Roberts was going was everywhere. The 1953 season is a good example. He began spring training at San Diego, but manager Lefty O'Doul pointed out that there were too many veteran players ahead of him, and the youngster was sent across country to Florida. And Florida became one of the rough spots along the way. The team

Dave Roberts with his first manager, renowned Negro League pitcher Chet Brewer. During the winter of 1951–52, Roberts, playing amateur baseball in his native Panama, was spotted by Brewer who was then managing a Panama professional team. When Brewer was hired to pilot a team in the States, Roberts was one of the players he wanted. (*Courtesy of Dave Roberts*)

Roberts was assigned to was Tampa, managed by fiery Ben Chapman, who had given Jackie Robinson a lot of grief a few years earlier.

Roberts played his heart out, gave it everything he had, and had a good spring, but was cut. He remembers one incident that happened in Plant City. He was on deck, watching the batter ahead of him, and the pitcher wound up and hit the batter in the head.

"We thought he was dead. He's the second hitter and I'm the third hitter. We go down there and they take him off the field, and I'm like, I haven't seen anybody get hit like that in my life. Ben Chapman looks me in the eye and says, 'Hey, dig in up there. Go in there swinging.' How do you tell a kid to dig in after he sees something like that? That guy was cold-blooded."

After being cut, Roberts figured it was time to forget about playing in the United States and go back to Panama, but teammate Lenny Pecou talked him out of it. Pecou, incredulous that Roberts had been cut, called the owner of the team in Grand Forks, North Dakota, and landed Roberts a spot on the roster. It seems a lot of people believed in him, and what each one talked about was his hitting. Earlier, in Porterville, Chet Brewer told the lefty about seeing him as an amateur back in Panama: "I saw that buggywhip you've got for a bat. I saw you whip the ball over the fence in right field."

So, thanks to Lenny Pecou, Roberts was about to complete a tour that in one season took him from Panama to southern California to Florida and Grand Forks, North Dakota—and it was still spring training. Roberts says that at the time if you'd asked him where North Dakota was, he wouldn't have had a clue; until the previous year Roberts had never even been outside of Panama.

After a slow start ("It was *cold*. I'm from the Tropics, man."), Roberts did fine and then had his contract purchased by Aberdeen, another Northern League club and an affiliate of the Baltimore Orioles. He had one of his most productive years in 1954 with Aberdeen, hitting 33 home runs and driving in 114 runs. He also stole 27 bases, a career high.

At this point in his career, Roberts thought he might not be very far away from a major league shot. "I started the season at Aberdeen, and I went to work, I went to town. And I kept saying, 'Maybe, just maybe . . .'" But it didn't happen. It didn't happen until 1962.

To better understand Roberts's journey, we need to roll back the clock. When he was a boy he climbed on top of a laundry building with some friends and watched an exhibition game that was the talk of Panama—Jackie Robinson and the Dodgers were playing. The year was 1947, and it was just before Robinson was going to go up to the majors. Roberts decided then and there, at age 13, that someday he'd play baseball in the major leagues.

Dave Roberts played for 13 minor league teams before he finally got called up to the majors. He can't say for sure why it took so long, but he believes it didn't help that he spent nearly three full seasons playing in San Antonio, where the wind blew in from right field, taking away his power and forcing him to try to push the ball to left field and center field. (Roberts was such a natural pull hitter that teams had occasionally used the shift on him, moving the shortstop over to the first base side of the diamond.)

But in 1962 Roberts was like a finely tuned machine. He found his stroke and was leading the American Association in hitting. In early September, Houston called him up to the big leagues.

"It was a dream come true. At last, after like nine or ten years, at last I'm here."

Roberts hit a line drive as a pinch hitter his first time up, and Bill Mazeroski caught the ball. The next night Pittsburgh was up by a run with two away in the ninth at Houston, and Roberts was sent up with runners on first and second:

> Elroy Face started me off with that fastball that ran away. He'd start it in the middle of the plate and it was supposed to run away, and I hit a bullet to left center for a double, and both guys scored. The ball game was over. Everybody was jumping up and down. I was standing at second base and Jim Pendleton came out and said, "Uh, Dave, come. You've done it. The game's over. You can come in now."

Roberts did very well the short time he played with Houston in 1962, driving in 10 of 13 runners who were in scoring position. He didn't win the American Association batting crown; Tommy McCraw inched ahead in September to overtake him, .326 to .322, but all in all 1962 was a banner year for the ballplayer from Panama.

At this point, we need to change gears, because the Dave Roberts story isn't just about baseball. Besides being an outstanding athlete, Roberts is someone with a unique outlook and a person who has abilities in many areas. He paints, reads about history and other subjects, and has never lost his fascination with the world and its people.

It was important to Roberts to make money in baseball in order to provide for his family and himself, but he also saw what he was doing as a type of exploring. He talks about listening to the radio as a kid and hearing about countries in the Caribbean where baseball was played. He later made a point to spend winters playing in different countries—Venezuela, Puerto Rico, Cuba, and Mexico—so he could expose himself to other cultures.

So in 1967, after being up and down from the majors to the minors a few times (and being named Minor League Player of the Year in 1965), when presented with an offer to play baseball in Japan, Roberts, after conferring with his wife, took the plunge and went ahead. He would be making more money than he would in the United States but also, as he says, "It was a new horizon."

While in Japan, Roberts wrote the following in his journal:

In February of 1967 a new phase of my life began. Jen, the kids, and I landed at Hanida International Airport. We went through the usual ritual that all the foreign ballplayers go through. I was told to lift my youngest child, just to show that I am a loving father. My wife held the other child—she was supposed to show some love too. We went through a press conference. I don't think I was very colorful, because I did not predict that I would lead the Central League in hitting, home runs, or RBIs. I wanted to wait and see how quickly I would adjust to Japanese life, and baseball.

Roberts and his family were provided with an apartment and assigned interpreters. Roberts, who grew up speaking Spanish and English and picked up a little French along the way, remarked that,

Japan was the only place I'd ever been in my entire life where language became a problem. I knew nothing, except *sayonora*. So I learned three words from the dictionary every day, without fail. And I would ask, "How do you use this? What is this

The Roberts family landing in Japan. (*Courtesy of Dave Roberts*)

sentence?" By the third year I was pretty good, could do my own interviews.

One of the first words I learned, on the ball field, relating to the ballplayers, was the word *abunai*, which means "danger." I wanted to be sure that the guys would not let me run into the fence. Early on, I almost ran into a fence. I was upset, turned around, the guy's standing right there. When the inning was over, I ran off the field and said to the interpreter, "Hey, you ask him why I almost ran into the fence and he didn't say a word." The interpreter said, "He would have said something but you wouldn't have understood it anyway." The Japanese logic is so precise. It is almost, how shall we say, unnerving.

As was the custom for over 30 years, each Japanese team was allowed to carry only two foreign-born players. Roberts's ally the first two years was Lou Jackson, a former Oriole and Cub. Jackson had played the previous year, and he clued in Roberts to many aspects of playing in Japan.

There were meetings and meetings and meetings and apologies for this and for that. At one point Roberts's team, the Sankei (later Yakult) Atoms, lost 12 straight games and the team owner felt such disgrace that he had the players face the stands before the next game and apologize to the fans.

Roberts says Jackson told him if he could make the adjustments and last until the end of June, he'd probably be able to handle playing in Japan. Otherwise, Jackson joked, "You're gonna lose your mind."

As it happened, Jackson and Roberts were playing alongside each other in the outfield one day in late June, when the Atom catcher, angry at a call, turned and slugged the umpire. Roberts ran over to Jackson, not sure he'd really seen what he'd just seen. Jackson smiled and reminded Roberts that he had to get used to weird stuff if he was going to last.

Roberts not only adjusted, he thrived. He arrived in Japan at age 34—which in those days was considered a year or two away from retirement for most ballplayers—but he was a young 34, and, by his own assessment, probably in the best shape of his life. He stayed for seven seasons and during that period was one of the top players in Japan. A leading power hitter, from 1967 through 1972 Roberts reached marks of 28, 40, 37, 19, 33, and 21 home runs.

After retiring in 1973 at age 40, Roberts and his family moved back to southern California, where they had resided before going to Japan.

Dave Roberts's team, the Sankei (later Yakult) Atoms, being blessed by a Shinto priest prior to the start of the 1967 Japanese baseball season. Roberts is in the back row. Teammate Lou Jackson, a former Cub and Oriole, is in the front row at right. (*Courtesy of Dave Roberts*)

He scouted for a year and then sold insurance until the economy turned sour. Then, during what may have been the most intense and important period of his life, he made a contribution that only he and those he touched can fully understand. He took a job "just to pay some bills" as a youth counselor and worked with some of the most troubled kids anywhere. He kept saying he was going to quit—his own kids begged him to quit—but he remained on the job. Soon after he began, Roberts realized how much help the youths needed. He buckled down and put his heart into his work. "I decided that my work there would be my ministry," he says. Roberts remained at the facility 12½ years, until a back injury forced him to quit.

Dave Roberts is reflective about many things, including his baseball career. He mentions playing with a young Brooks Robinson at San Antonio in 1956: "He threw the ball soft; you could catch it with your bare hands." He talks about playing with Luis Aparicio for three years in Venezuela and, while in the big leagues, facing fireballers such as Jim Maloney, Bob Veale, and Sandy Koufax. He tells about Orlando Cepeda and a friend from Panama, Jackie Brathwaite, who gave him valuable advice along the way, and he remembers how when he was a youngster in the Texas League, some fans in rival towns were so cutting with racial insults that "I couldn't get in the dugout fast enough."

Roberts played with and against thousands of players, including fading Negro League stars such as Willard Brown and Buzz Clarkson in the Texas League. Before he was through, he would bat against the top pitchers in Japan and compete on the field against Sadaharu Oh and other Japanese stars. He played baseball in nine countries, for teams such as the Louisville Colonels, the Oklahoma City 89ers, and the Houston Buffaloes as well as the Kintetsu Buffaloes and Cerveza Balboa.

When he looks back, he often thinks about Chet Brewer, who gave him advice on many things. It was Brewer who told a young Dave Roberts, "Wherever you play, always play so you can be invited back." Says Roberts, "Every town that I've played, I can go back and say, 'I played here thirty years ago.' The reaction would be, 'Yes, we probably remember you,' or, 'You were . . . there was nothing negative.' What I'm saying, there's nothing like, 'Now you're here, now we can run you out of town, like we should have back then.' Austin, I can go back to and Knoxville and Aberdeen and the other places."

A top player in Japan for six years, Dave Roberts connects in a game against the Tokyo Giants. (*Courtesy of Dave Roberts*)

Roberts didn't make a big splash in the major leagues, but that doesn't mean he wasn't a fine ballplayer. He certainly is someone worth knowing about, someone worth remembering. His numbers from 22 years in baseball (not counting winter ball) are 2,809 games, 2,660 hits, 1,639 runs, 429 home runs, and 1,593 RBIs.

David Leonard Roberts

Born June 30, 1933, Panama City, Republic of Panama
Batted left, threw left. Height: 6'. Weight: 172 lbs.

Year	Club	League	G	AB	R	H	2B	3B	HR	RBI	SB	BA
1952	Porterville	Southwest International	80	290	98	91	15	4	10	40	20	.314
1953	Grand Forks	Northern	126	465	89	125	20	1	15	88	13	.269
1954	Aberdeen	Northern	135	499	114	148	28	7	33	114	27	.297
1955	San Antonio	Texas	153	488	71	113	22	6	14	84	10	.232
1956	San Antonio	Texas	147	539	109	148	28	9	7	67	6	.275
1957	Vancouver	Pacific Coast	1	1	0	0	0	0	0	0	0	.000
1957	Knoxville	South Atlantic	44	153	24	46	6	2	5	22	1	.301
1957	San Antonio/Austin	Texas	99	347	50	89	12	4	5	36	7	.256
1958	Austin	Texas	148	521	96	153	19	6	20	61	4	.294
1959	Louisville	American Association	133	385	59	97	20	2	10	50	5	.252
1960	Sacramento	Pacific Coast	9	37	6	9	3	1	1	4	0	.243
1960	Austin	Texas	55	205	40	63	13	2	9	41	2	.307
1960	Dallas–Fort Worth	American Association	71	235	26	56	7	2	4	18	3	.238
1961	Jacksonville	South Atlantic	77	266	50	84	18	2	8	29	2	.316
1961	Houston	American Association	41	130	20	27	5	1	3	21	0	.208
1962	Oklahoma City	American Association	133	481	86	155	38*	8	15	96	3	.322
1962	Houston	National	16	53	3	13	3	0	1	10	0	.245
1963	Oklahoma City	Pacific Coast	151	507	82	137	24	5	16	86	1	.270
1964	Oklahoma City	Pacific Coast	38	132	32	49	17	3	5	30	0	.371
1964	Houston	National	61	125	9	23	4	1	1	7	0	.184
1965	Oklahoma City	Pacific Coast	144	493	102	157	20	6	38*	114	8	.318

David Leonard Roberts (*continued*)

Year	Club	League	G	AB	R	H	2B	3B	HR	RBI	SB	BA
1966	Columbus	International	119	408	67	111	14	2	26	83	0	.272
1966	Pittsburgh	National	14	16	3	2	1	0	0	0	0	.125
1967	Sankei Atoms	Central (Japan)	126	459	72	124	26	2	28	89	2	.270
1968	Sankei Atoms	Central	128	456	82	135	12	2	40	94	4	.296
1969	Sankei Atoms	Central	116	424	72	135	18	0	37	95	5	.318
1970	Yakult Atoms	Central	124	420	43	100	22	0	19	52	1	.238
1971	Yakult Atoms	Central	128	452	63	121	20	1	33	76	8	.268
1972	Yakult Atoms	Central	120	383	55	106	22	1	22	63	2	.277
1973	Yakult Atoms	Central	36	115	13	29	5	2	2	16	0	.252
1973	Kintetsu Buffaloes	Pacific	36	65	3	14	0	0	2	7	0	.215
		Major League totals	91	194	15	38	8	1	2	17		.196
		Japanese totals	814	2774	403	764	124	8	183	492		.275
		Minor League totals	1904	6582	1221	1858	329	73	244	1084		.282
		Combined totals–22 years	2809	9550	1639	2660	461	82	429	1593		—

*Led league

5

THE DUTCH MASTER

LARRY JANSEN

Larry Jansen averaged 19 wins a season for his first five years in the major leagues. His record from 1947 through 1951 was 96 and 56, with an ERA of 3.33. Then injuries took their toll, and Jansen's effectiveness dropped off.

Larry Jansen is credited with being one of the pitchers to popularize the use of the slider in the major leagues. In the minors, he was the last pitcher to win 30 or more games at the Triple A level. He was the last pitcher ever to face Joe DiMaggio; the last player to pitch more than four innings in an All-Star game. And most important historically, he was the winning pitcher on the day Bobby Thomson hit the Shot Heard 'Round the World.

Larry Jansen lives 20 miles from Portland, Oregon, in the Tualatin Valley, an area known for farming.

LARRY JANSEN: I was born and raised here in Verboort. It was a Dutch community then. Now it's more mixed.

The crops around here vary. We grow a lot of strawberries. We grow wheat and all kinds of fruit—peaches and pears and apples. We have an awful lot of nursery farmers. When I was young we milked a lot of cows.

So I was a farm boy. I pitched semipro ball on Sundays. A year or so after high school, the Red Sox heard about me and sent a scout here. The scout liked what he saw, and he signed me to what was then called a *blank contract.* I didn't know where I was going to go, who I was going to play for. It was a Red Sox contract, but no team was listed.

The next spring I didn't receive a contract, didn't get any information at all. So I didn't know what to do. I knew an umpire in Portland who had umpired a lot of our semipro games out here, and I gave him a call. He said, "Well, I've got Judge Landis's address; wire Landis and see what he says." I wired Landis, and Landis wired back immediately that I was a free agent.

I ended up signing with the San Francisco Seals, and they assigned me to Salt Lake City in the Pioneer League. That was 1940, and I ended up winning 20 games and leading the league in earned run average. The reason I did well wasn't necessarily because of the amount of stuff I had, because I wasn't very fast. But I had excellent control. That's what San Francisco liked about me. The one thing that they were skeptical about was that I was so thin. I only weighed about 155 pounds. I was a skinny kid.

I pitched for the Seals in 1941 and had a good year, but in 1942 I was having a rough time, and Larry Woodall, one of our coaches, taught me the slider. The slider was not a common pitch in those days. Very few pitchers threw it. Larry Woodall had been a catcher, and I have no idea where he learned the pitch.

The slider is really a great pitch. You hold your fingers a little to the side, turn the wrist to the left, and with the proper release the ball spirals like a football. Sometimes it will break two inches, sometimes six inches. That's one of the reasons it's so effective. The batter can't tell what it's going to do. To most batters it looks like a fastball is coming, and they can't pull the string in time. If they hit it, they usually top it. You get a lot of ground balls with the slider.

I had a hard time mastering the slider. I threw it on the sidelines for six weeks before I ever used it in a game, and it wasn't too effective. But during the war I was up here in Oregon, farming, and I had some opportunities to throw the slider playing semipro ball. I played semipro ball about twice a week, and I mastered the slider real well. When I went back with the Seals the last part of '45 I was a much better pitcher than before. I won four games and lost one, and the Seals made it into the playoffs. I wasn't eligible for the playoffs, but they voted me a full share for helping to get them in.

Larry Jansen (*Courtesy of The Topps Company, Inc.*)

We had a terrific ball club in 1946. Ferris Fain was there, and besides being a great hitter he was a big help in the field, very agile. Roy Nicely was the shortstop, and he could hound the ball as well as anybody. And of course it was great playing for Lefty O'Doul. We won the pennant and set a minor league attendance record that year. We were drawing so many people that the Oakland and San Francisco clubs got together and decided to split the Sunday doubleheaders—a game in one city in the morning, a game in the other city in the afternoon.

Of course the players didn't want to do it and neither did O'Doul. The first time they tried it was on Easter Sunday. They scheduled the first game for 10:15 A.M. in San Francisco, and O'Doul said there'd only be a couple thousand people in the stands and "that'll put an end to that." Who wanted to play ball games in two different cities in one day?

So I went out and warmed up at about 5 minutes to 10, and there were 10,000 people in the stands! So the rest of that year that's the way we played 'em on Sundays—one game in Oakland and one game in San Francisco.

I won 30 games for the Seals in 1946. I was hitting the ball well and that helped me win some ball games—because O'Doul left me in to hit for myself instead of taking me out for a pinch hitter. A couple of those games we won in the late innings and I was fortunate I was still in the game. But I did pitch well that year. My earned run average was 1.47, which is the Coast League record.

The Seals had a working agreement with the New York Giants. That's how we ended up with Cliff Melton and some of the others. The Seals traded me to the Giants for two players. I don't want to dwell too much on this, but I had an agreement that I would get 10 percent of the sale price if I was sold to a big league club. Since I was traded instead of sold, that deal was off. I don't want to knock the Seals, because they had a good organization, but things like that make a player a little cautious.

When the Giants sent me a contract for 1947 it wasn't for hardly anything, and I sent it back. So I ended up reporting late. When I got to spring training I saw the Giants had quite a few pitchers in camp. They had finished last the year before and they wanted to look at a lot of young pitchers, and most of them were younger than me. I was one of the old guys. I was almost 27. Another thing that hurt was that the last couple of pitchers the Seals had sent up had done very poorly. So I wasn't a sure thing with the Giants, and I was wondering if I was going to get much of a chance to play.

The first game I pitched for the Giants in spring training was against the Cleveland Indians in Tucson. Bob Feller pitched for the Indians, and about the third inning he was up and he hit a line drive back at me. There were a lot of white shirts in the crowd, and the sun was reflecting off of them, and I never saw the ball. It broke my cheek.

I missed a couple of weeks, and when I came back the season was almost ready to start. I got into three games, pitched about six innings as a reliever, and I did very poorly.

The cut-down time was a little different back then. I think we had 30 days to carry extra players. So I had until about the middle of May to make the club. The bull pen coach, Hank Gowdy—we always called him Mr. Gowdy—liked me quite a bit, and he went to Mel Ott and said, "Why don't you give this boy a start before the cut-down time?" He knew I had never relieved in my life and he pointed that out to Ott.

So they did. They started me on the tenth of May against the Braves, and I won against Red Barrett. About four days later they had me scheduled to pitch against the Cardinals in St. Louis. Luckily we had whirlpools in those days. I spent a day or two in the whirlpool to lose some of my stiffness and soreness, and I went seven innings against the Cardinals and beat them. So I survived the cut, and then I went on from there. So I actually didn't start a game until the tenth of May, and I ended up winning 20 games.

Walker Cooper was my catcher, and he helped me quite a bit. He knew all the hitters. He'd give me a sign, but I'd shake my head. He'd come right back with the same sign and nod his head, "Yes. Throw it." When the inning was over he'd come over and say, "You dummy, you let me call the game. You just pitch it." He knew how the hitters should be pitched to. I learned a lot from him.

The Giants had a bunch of sluggers in those days—Cooper, Johnny Mize, Willard Marshall, Sid Gordon. Then Leo Durocher came in and made some trades. He wanted Durocher-type players. More speed. Hit and run. Hit to the opposite field. We traded with the Braves before the 1950 season and got Alvin Dark and Eddie Stanky for Willard Marshall, Sid Gordon, Buddy Kerr, and a pitcher by the name of Sam Webb.

The trades made us a lot better defensively, a lot quicker—especially in the outfield. It means a lot to you as a pitcher when you see a fielder get to a ball that before would have fallen in for a hit. That's one reason my earned-run average was lower that year. I gave up fewer hits. And we turned more double plays. Buddy Kerr was an excellent shortstop, but Dark and Stanky came as a package; they worked real well together.

I was on the All-Star team in 1950, and Burt Shotton told me before the game that I'd pitch the last three innings "regardless of what happens."

I entered the game in the seventh, and I pitched real hard because my spot in the batting order is coming up, and I figure I'll be taken out for a pinch hitter, since we're down a run. I struck out a couple of guys and then he let me hit for myself, which really surprised me. So then I pitched the eighth inning figuring it would be my last, and I struck out a couple of more guys. Ralph Kiner homered in the top of the ninth for us and tied the game. I went out to pitch the bottom of the ninth and I just let her fly again. I struck out two more batters.

Shotton let me hit for myself in the tenth inning. And I'm thinking, "How long is this going to go on?" So I settled back and started pitching to people just to get them out, on ground balls or fly outs. Before that, I was throwing hard because I thought each inning was my last.

Burt Shotton had a lot of confidence in me, and he wanted the National League to win that game awful bad. Because the American League, if you look back, had dominated the National League up to that point.

I ended up pitching five innings. Gave up one hit and didn't walk anybody. Ewell Blackwell came in for us in the 12th, and Red Schoendienst got Burt Shotton his win in the 14th, when he hit a home run.

The next year is the year everybody remembers—1951. We were so far behind in August, something like 13½ games behind Brooklyn. We were in second place, and you think that's where you're going to finish.

And then we put together a 16-game winning streak. All of a sudden we're 4 or 5 games out, with maybe 20 or 30 games left. So now we were starting to think, "Hey, we can catch these guys." And I'm the guy who's always saying, "No, no, hey, guys, there's not enough games left, and if the Dodgers don't lose, we can't possibly catch them."

But we kept winning and they lost enough games, and then we were tied. We tied them on Saturday when Sal Maglie beat the Braves. So there was one game left in the season. I was scheduled to pitch it, and if we won we'd have at least a tie. And of course if we won and the Dodgers lost, we'd be the champs.

Well, I'd been having some back trouble. So when I went to warm up, the trainer and the team physician were there. I don't know if the adrenaline was going or what, but I didn't feel any pain at all. I told them, "Hell, I'm ready to go."

We went into the ninth leading the Braves 3–1. I was a fast worker and the game was moving along. The first guy up for them in the ninth got a double and he scored. Then there was a ball that could have been a double-play ball to end the game, but Stanky got spiked and only got one out on it. Leo came out and ran over to Stanky, and as he passed the mound he hollers to me, "Hey, are you alright?" "Hell, yes," I told him. Leo left me in the game, and then Willard Marshall flew out. Game over.

Meanwhile, the Dodgers and the Phillies have a wild game going. Jackie Robinson makes a great play in the 12th inning, and then the Dodgers win it in 14 innings. But we don't know this. We don't know we have a playoff tomorrow in Brooklyn until we're halfway back to New York by train. So instead of celebrating—our champagne is on the train—we can't drink a drop because we have a playoff game to play tomorrow.

When we got off the train in New York, there were a lot of people there, but we've got to get home and get some sleep.

We played the Dodgers Monday, Tuesday, and Wednesday. The first game was in Brooklyn, and Jim Hearn pitched a great game for us. The second and third games were in New York. Clem Labine shut us out 10–0 in the second game, and everyone knows how the third game turned out.

Sal Maglie got into trouble early in the game, but he settled down and pitched a great game. Leo had me warming up in the first inning, but he didn't put me in until the top of the ninth. Of course, the score was 4–1 Dodgers. Newcombe was pitching a very strong ball game. I figured it was all over, of course. I just wanted to get

The most important pitching assignment of Larry Jansen's career came on the last day of the 1951 season and resulted in his twenty-second win, an opportunity to play the Brooklyn Dodgers in a three-game playoff, and a kiss on the cheek from manager Leo Durocher. (*AP/Wide World Photos*)

them out and get it over with. I thought it was time to pack our bags and go home.

During our rally in the bottom of the inning, Mueller got hurt sliding into third base, and they had to carry him off the field. So there was a lot of time for Dressen to make up his mind about what he wanted to do, if he wanted to leave Newcombe in or bring in a reliever.

Thomson came back and sat down on the bench, just to relax a little bit. He later said he was telling himself, "Don't be in hurry. Don't be anxious. Relax. Wait, wait, wait."

There's been a lot said about what took place on the mound, about Reese telling Dressen, "Newcombe's taken us this far," and so forth. When I saw they were bringing in Ralph Branca I thought maybe we had a chance after all. Because I knew Thomson always hit Branca well. I was sitting next to Bobby in the dugout. I said, "Bobby, here comes your boy."

Bobby took the first pitch for a called strike, and I thought, "Oh, my gosh!" It was right in his wheelhouse, belt high, a fastball, right down the middle, and he took it! I guess the next pitch—the one he hit out—was actually a bad pitch. It was high. He tomahawked that ball.

So 1951 was quite a year. We won our last 7 games, 12 of our last 13, and 37 of our last 44. That's what it took to tie the Dodgers.

We lost to the Yankees in the World Series, but there's no crime in that. We played well. And even though we lost I consider it quite a thrill. They had Mantle batting leadoff. He was something special. He could really fly. He dragged a bunt off me that was impossible to stop. Nothing you could do about the way he bunted.

In the last game, I was the last pitcher on the mound for the Giants. So when Joe DiMaggio batted for his final time as a professional, it was against me. He got a double.

The next couple of years I had a lot of trouble with my back, and that led to me hurting my arm. I was on the inactive list when we swept Cleveland in the '54 Series. After that I went back to the Pacific Coast League and played until 1960, but I also was a pitching coach. That was my second career in baseball.

In 1961 Alvin Dark asked me to be his pitching coach when he became manager of the San Francisco Giants. As it happens, I was all set to become manager of Portland that year; but I went with the Giants instead. I spent II years with the Giants in that capacity. I worked with Gaylord Perry and Juan Marichal, Jack Sanford, Bob Bolin, Billy O'Dell, Frank Linzy—a lot of good pitchers.

The best thing I did for Marichal was leave him alone. He knew how to pitch, and the only thing I ever did with Marichal was made sure he stayed in shape, and if he asked me a question or two, I would try to help him. He had so many pitches. He could throw overhand, sidearm. He had a great screwball. He threw hard and he had tremendous control.

I can remember a game in which Marichal beat Spahn 1–0 in 16 innings. They both pitched the entire game. Willie Mays won it with a home run in the bottom of the 16th. It was a night game, and the next afternoon I was out there during batting practice, running the pitchers, and somebody hit a ball down by the runway, where the players enter the field. Spahn was just walking in and he picks up the ball *and he throws it all the way out to second base.* After pitching 16 innings the night before. And he's my age! I said to myself, "My arm would have fallen off."

Another game that stands out from that period was pitched by Gaylord Perry. Perry didn't do real well at first, but then we had a game in New York that was very important to his career. We beat the Mets in the first game of a doubleheader and then the second game went into extra innings. Perry went in as a reliever and he just kept going. He pitched 9 or 10 innings in relief. That showed he had what it took. We won the game in the 23rd inning when Del Crandall got a pinch hit. I believe Tom Haller caught that whole game, all 23 innings.

In 1971 the Giants let me go. I guess they thought it was time for a change. The day I learned I was fired I called a friend of mine with the Cubs and told him I was just let go by the Giants and he said, "Don't sign with anybody until you get through talking with us." It turned out I was unemployed for one day. So I worked two years in Chicago—with Leo Durocher and then Whitey Lockman.

I was fortunate to have more than 20 years in by then for my pension, and that's meant an awful lot to my family. So when I retired after the 1973 season, it was time. I was ready to retire from baseball, ready to try other things.

◆ ◆ ◆

The first time Larry Jansen told me about getting hit by a line drive in 1947 he brushed over it rather quickly. I later asked him to give me the details, and it turned out to be a rather gruesome story. For those who want to know just how rough of a sport baseball really is, read on.

The sun was shining on the people in the stands, and they were sitting there in short sleeves and white shirts. It was really tough to see a ball coming out of there, a ball coming off the bat, and this was a line drive. So I just never did see it.

It knocked me down, and the ball went out to right field, and they had to come and get me. I don't know if I lost consciousness or not. I don't think so.

They took me in the clubhouse, and of course they called an ambulance, and then while this was going on—the next half inning—Hank Edwards, the right fielder, dove for a ball and dislocated his shoulder.

So the first ambulance gets there, and they decided that I wasn't hurt so bad. And I thought, "Wait a minute," and I felt a hole in my face.

And they said, "No, no, you're alright. You've got a bad bruise." And of course my eyes were swelled shut and I was a mess.

But they took Hank Edwards first, because they said, "He's dislocated his shoulder, so we'll send him in the first ambulance, and we've already called another ambulance, so we'll put Jansen in the second ambulance."

So the second ambulance gets there and takes me to the hospital, and Hank Edwards hasn't arrived yet. They took him to the wrong hospital. So they had to bring him to the hospital where I was.

All this time I'm laying there on the stretcher. And they bring Edwards in and put him on the table, and knock him out.

And then they're going to put his arm back in place. One doctor looked like he put his knee on Hank's chest and grabbed his arm and started pulling—wrapping it around and around—so it'd pop back in the socket.

Now I'm lying there watching this, and finally somebody said, "Hey, get that young fella out of here. I don't want him to see all this."

So they took me out. Then they moved me in, x-rayed me, and the doctor came back. Not talking directly to me, talking to the assistant, he said, "We're going to have to operate on this kid right now, because his face is all broken to pieces." That scared the hell out of me. I'm laying right there listening to it.

"How bad am I hurt?"

"Well, we're going to have to operate. We're going to have to put some bones back in place. Your cheekbone is shattered." So that's what they had to do.

What they did, the doctor told me later, they operated up through my mouth, and he said they took a little bit of steel rod—it was about a quarter of an inch in diameter—and just pushed it up in there. And with their hands on the outside, they tried to feel where all the bones were and started pushing things around in there, hoping that the bones would get into the right spots where they would mend together.

So that night they told me after I had come to, "Now, young man, if you don't roll on this tonight we won't have to put a brace on it to keep the bones from moving." But instead of putting some-one in there with me, or something, they just left me there. That's the way it was in those days.

The next day they x-rayed me again and the doctor said, "You're lucky. None of the bone chips seem to have moved. Your face should be good enough by tonight where you shouldn't be able to move them around."

And that's the way it was. I was very lucky. They said if it had hit me a half inch higher or so it would have knocked my eye out. Hazards of the game.

Lawrence (Larry) Joseph Jansen

Born July 16, 1920, Verboort, OR.
Batted right, threw right. Height: 6' 2". Weight: 190 lbs.

Year	Club	League	G	IP	W	L	Pct.	R	H	ER	SO	BB	ERA
1940	Salt Lake City	Pioneer	31	214	20	7	.741*	82	194	52	148	69	2.19*
1941	San Francisco	Pacific Coast	32	238	16	10	.615	97	220	74	70	75	2.80
1942	San Francisco	Pacific Coast	32	173	11	14	.440	108	222	83	46	39	4.32
1943–44							(voluntarily retired)						
1945	San Francisco	Pacific Coast	7	55	4	1	.800	25	63	25	34	12	4.09
1946	San Francisco	Pacific Coast	38	321	30*	6	.833	85	254	56	171	69	1.57*
1947	New York	National	42	248	21	5	.808	102	241	87	104	57	3.16
1948	New York	National	42	277	18	12	.600	125	283	111	126	54	3.61
1949	New York	National	37	260	15	16	.484	130	271	111	113	62	3.84
1950	New York	National	40	275	19	13	.594	106	238	92	161	55	3.01
1951	New York	National	39	279	23*	11	.676	102	254	94	145	56	3.03
1952	New York	National	34	167	11	11	.500	91	183	76	74	47	4.10
1953	New York	National	36	185	11	16	.407	96	185	85	88	55	4.14
1954	New York	National	13	41	2	2	.500	32	57	27	15	15	5.93
1955	Seattle	Pacific Coast	26	137	7	7	.500	55	147	51	66	26	3.34
1956	Seattle	Pacific Coast	24	98	11	2	.846	33	85	28	59	20	2.58
1956	Cincinnati	National	8	35	2	3	.400	20	39	20	16	9	5.14
1957	Seattle	Pacific Coast	30	180	10	12	.455	70	185	63	82	25	3.16
1958	Portland	Pacific Coast	22	158	9	10	.474	57	142	55	85	24	3.13

Lawrence (Larry) Joseph Jansen (continued)

Year	Club	League	G	IP	W	L	Pct.	R	H	ER	SO	BB	ERA
1959	Portland	Pacific Coast	11	24	1	0	1.000	10	26	7	11	4	2.62
1960	Portland	Pacific Coast	9	18	3	0	1.000	5	11	3	13	6	1.50
		Major League totals	291	1767	122	89	.578	804	1751	703	842	410	3.58
		Minor League totals	262	1616	122	69	.639	627	1549	497	785	369	2.77
		Combined totals—19 years	553	3383	244	158	.607	1431	3300	1200	1627	779	3.19

World Series Record

Year	Club	League	G	IP	W	L	Pct.	R	H	ER	SO	BB	ERA
1951	New York	National	3	10	0	2	.000	7	8	7	5	4	6.30

All-Star Game Record

Year	League	IP	W	L	Pct.	R	H	ER	SO	BB	ERA
1950	National	5	0	0	.000	0	1	0	6	0	0.00

*Led league

6

UNSER CHOE

JOE HAUSER

When I was a boy my best friend Steve Hollenberg, his dad Leo, and I would sometimes play catch. Mr. Hollenberg would throw his usual assortment of junk—knuckler, curve, slip pitch. Every once in a while he'd switch his glove to his right hand and toss a few left-handed. It was amidst the pines of the Feather River Park Resort that we did our ball tossing. Every summer in the mid- and late '60s I spent a week with the Hollenbergs at that quiet northern California vacation spot.

Leo Hollenberg was my biggest baseball influence when I was a kid. I loved talking baseball with him. I remember when he told me about Joe Hauser. We were playing catch; it was dusk. In a little while we would go into our cabin for dinner.

I can't remember exactly what Mr. Hollenberg said about Hauser, but I distinctly recall there was a reverential tone in his voice when he talked about the former slugger. I've since learned that Hauser, a well-known name throughout the country in the 1930s, '40s, and '50s, holds a special place in the hearts and memories of many fans familiar with baseball of an earlier era.

Sitting at my desk, I looked through the Baseball Encyclopedia. I double-checked Hauser's birth date: he would be 92 years old. I dialed directory assistance for Sheboygan, Wisconsin, the town Hauser retired to, and was given a number. Not knowing what to expect, I made the call and was greeted with a booming hello from a voice, deep and full, like no other I've ever heard.

"What's on your mind, coach?" said Hauser.

I told him about my book and he agreed to be interviewed. We talked for nearly two hours that day. I was fortunate to talk with him several more times before he passed away in 1997. Humorous at times but also serious and proud, Hauser could also be described as being full of mischief. Once he greeted me with, "Where you calling from? The police station?" It seemed a strange question and then I got the punch line: "They'll throw you in jail for talking to me!"

I heard terms from Hauser I'd never heard before. If he wasn't sure you had caught his drift, he'd follow up a statement with a gentle bark, "Grab me?" Another endearing trait, if he liked what you had said, his old voice would bellow an affirmative, "Yaaaah!"

There was one particular greeting that I found rather memorable. "What do you want to talk about?" he once asked. "Baseball? Or pussy?"

Joe Hauser's career started a long time ago, before the Black Sox Scandal, before Babe Ruth had become an everyday outfielder. Here's the story of one of baseball's true legendary figures, in his own words.

JOE HAUSER: I started when I was 13. I played in a saloon league in Milwaukee. The name of the team was Zunker's Comers. That means, "We're a team, and we're coming along!" I'm one year older than the year, so that would be 1912. There was a little two-lane bowling alley in Zunker's saloon, and I set pins for three cents a game. When I worked there, the alleys were about 50 years old then. I'd pick up a quarter, 50 cents a night. He had all those old fogeys bowling there.

They used to call me "Zip," on account of my fastball. I'd strike out 15, 17, 18 a game. If I struck out 12 I didn't have nothing. I only lost one game in four years and the team in Waupun asked me to pitch for them. It was close to Milwaukee, and I said yes. It was semipro, big league stuff compared to what I was used to. There were guys on that team 25, 35 years old. Some had been minor leaguers who quit when they didn't move up. I was 18, just a pup.

That year I won 12 games and didn't lose any, and we went to the state tournament. I was fast enough to get the batters scared at the plate. I pitched a shutout, two to nothing, and we won the championship. That was a big deal in those days. I got recommended to Connie Mack, the Philadelphia manager. In 1918 I went to spring training with the Athletics in Jacksonville, Florida.

It was the biggest thrill I could get, to go to spring training with a big league club. I was down there about two weeks, and all I had in my hands was a bat. I wasn't doing any pitching. So one day, Connie Mack says, "Joe, I'm taking you out to the ballpark tomorrow morning. I'm going to look you over, see what you've got."

He took me out to the ballpark, he and I and a catcher, that's all that was there, and I was scared to death. That was too big a jump. Hell, I had been pitching on the sandlots.

He took me out. I was wilder than hell. We left the ballpark, went back to the hotel. A day or two later he says, "Joe, I'm going to send you home." He paid my freight back, and gave me a hundred dollars. So I was back home in Milwaukee for 1918. The manager of the Milwaukee team liked me. He was from Providence, and he signed me to a contract. He wanted me to play in Providence for a while—that was a Class A league at that time—which was good baseball. Then I would switch over to the Milwaukee Brewers in a year or so.

I joined the Providence club in New Haven, middle of the season. It was June. The second day I was there the manager, who was a hell of a nice guy, put me in to pitch. I started the game and walked two batters. I struck out two and then I walked another guy to load the bases. The manager came in from left field, where he was playing, and he took me out of the game. I never pitched again.

But they knew I had a bat. I always was a good hitter. I went to the outfield and hit about .270.

Hauser played a full season for Providence in 1919, hitting .273 and leading the league with 21 triples. His hometown club, the American Association's Milwaukee Brewers—the team that owned his contract—called him back for the 1920 season. He played right field.

You play a game in Milwaukee, and if you have a bad day, they ride the hell out of you. So, one game, I was up and I struck out, and they gave me the razzberry. And my fans there, they said, "Don't get on him, that's Unser Choe." *Unser Choe* is German. It means Our Joe. That's how I got the nickname Unser Choe.

There was a game I remember, it was either 1920 or '21. Jack Egan, our manager, was coaching at third base. I was batting with two men on and nobody out. I looked at Egan to get the sign. Do I sacrifice or do I swing away? What does he want me to do? I take my look and he has the bunt sign on, but he also is giving me the sign to hit away. I decide to hit and I hit the ball out of the park. He told me he had the bunt sign on, and I told him he had both signs on, and I chose to hit. He said he was glad I hit the home run but said the next time he would give the signs better.

In 1921 the Brewers trained in Gulfport, Mississippi. We had a game in Bogalusa, Louisiana. You had to go through New Orleans to get there. The manager told me, "We're going to stop in New Orleans at a sport shop and get you a first baseman's glove. If you can make the plays at first base, which I think you can—you've got a good pair of hands, you've got a good bat—you'll be in the big leagues in one year." And that's just what happened.

The game in Bogalusa was against the St. Louis Browns, and George Sisler was the Browns' first baseman. I'm picking up all the little tips I can about tagging the guy, how to cover the bag, things like that. I'm holding a guy on, and the pitcher throws the ball over to me, and I turn to my left to tag him. Sisler hollered to me from the bench, "You turn the other way, Joe," to my right. "That's where the runner is!"

So I make those mistakes once, but that's the only time I make mistakes like that. I picked up fast, and I had a good year at the plate. They sold my contract to the Philadelphia Athletics.

Connie Mack was pretty sure on me. He came over to Milwaukee one day to see me play when the Athletics were in Chicago. Somebody told me he was there, and I got four hits, including a home run. That sold the deal. The Athletics paid $50,000 and gave up four good ballplayers to get me.

I felt at home in the big leagues. I wasn't scared like when I was pitching in New Haven. I got a chance to play and I had a pretty good year. I was listening all the time, trying to learn what I could.

Joe hit .323 for Philadelphia in 1922 and followed that up with a .307 average in 1923. His power was starting to show; he hit 16 home runs and had 94 RBIs. His average fell off a little in 1924 to .288, but he was blossoming as a power bitter. He drove in 115 runs and belted 27 home runs, which was second in the American League to Babe Ruth.

On August 2, 1924, Joe Hauser had three homers and a double, which translates into 14 total bases—an American League record at that time.

The double was hit harder than any of the home runs. I hit my double to deep right center, about 365 feet. It was hit like a bullet and hit near the top of a high screen on top of the fence. Six inches higher, and it would have been over. Speaker caught it off the screen.

Ty Cobb broke my record. He had three homers, a double, and two singles for 16 total bases. Six for six. Not a bad day.

One time, against Boston, Jack Quinn was pitching for the Red Sox and I hit a home run with two out in the ninth to win the game. Quinn wasn't too happy about it. He was traded to the Athletics later and he came up to me. "You son of a bitch," he said. "I'll never forget that home run you hit off me in Boston." But he had a big smile on his face. Nice guy. Used to give me cigars if he was pitching and I drove in a couple of runs.

Walter Johnson was the best in the business. He never threw at anybody. And he was a good batter for a pitcher. He'd hit one out of the park against you once in a while. He'd give me a nice "Hello, Joe!" when I saw him on the field.

I had a pitcher hit me one time in Philadelphia. Hit me in the butt. I never argued with a pitcher about a knockdown pitch. Because if they throw the ball high, they never would hit me. I was very agile at shuffling and ducking my head. So one day I get hit in my butt. Halfway to first I said, "Hey, pitcher, if that leaves a mark, I'll buy you dinner!" I was so sociable.

Joe had a good spring in 1925 and the Athletics came north to play a series of exhibition games against the Phillies, just before the season was to begin.

We were in the field. I was playing back. The batter hits the ball to short and I run to first. But I don't get there. I got about halfway, and down I went. My kneecap was broken. I don't know why it happened. They put wire in it to hold it together.

The knee was in two pieces and I was out for the season. Along in August when the club was on the road I was working out a little—just jogging a bit. One day after about three or four weeks the wires that held the bones together snapped. I heard it. I saw the doctor and he said, "So long as the wires don't break through we won't worry about it." I never had the kneecap replaced. It's still in there. So are the wires. Last year I got kind of a twitch in my wired knee. I was feeling for the wire. It's still in there.

After missing the 1925 season, the next year I still wasn't right. Connie Mack had me batting cleanup. He was hoping I'd come out of it, but I never did. I ended up hitting .190.

Joe was optioned to Kansas City in the American Association for 1927, and he was his old self again.

I had a great year. Lots of extra-base hits. Batted .353. I was a better hitter than I ever was.

The old Kansas City ballpark was mammoth. The right field fence was 400 feet away and 30 feet high. Batters didn't even think about trying to hit home runs there. You don't jump across the Grand Canyon, and you don't hit home runs in Kansas City.

I never thought I'd hit one out, but I did. It was on a Saturday. Nobody had ever hit a home run there before, and they passed the hat. Some guy with a megaphone went around the grandstand and collected about $250 for me.

The next day, I was up, and I hit a bullet. I started to run, and then I slowed down a little. Did that ball leave the park? I couldn't believe it. Another homer. They passed the hat again and I got another couple hundred dollars.

Hauser mentioned that he hit balls in smaller parks that travelled as far as the ones he hit in Kansas City, but because the fences were shorter they didn't get as much attention.

The Athletics picked up the option on Hauser's contract and he was back for another shot in '28. Joe started strong but faded later and ended the season hitting .260. It was during that season that Ty Cobb and Tris Speaker, suspected of being part of a plot to fix a ball game, were both sold to the A's.

Cobb and Speaker were on the Athletics with me, but I didn't talk too much to them. Speaker was OK, but Cobb was a son of a bitch. Nobody liked him. There were only two ballplayers at his funeral. He played dirty. He'd go into a base with his spikes high, legs in the air. Players were afraid of him. Who wouldn't be?

One time we needed a pinch hitter and Connie Mack says to Cobb, "Ty, can you hit this pitcher?" Cobb stood up and said, "I can hit any pitcher who ever lived!" Mack says, "Fine. Hauser, grab a bat."

Babe Ruth was a nice guy. The biggest attraction baseball's ever had. He got a lot of walks, so I saw him a lot at first base.

I can't say too much about Ruth, Gehrig, Simmons, and the other stars. They were great ballplayers. They could do everything right. And they were all tough. When they got up to that dish, they were tough.

Jimmie Foxx became the Athletics' full-time first baseman in 1929, and Hauser was optioned to Milwaukee. Later that season the Cleveland Indians purchased Hauser's contract.

Hauser was back in the big leagues, but it was a mixed blessing. Cleveland already had a stand-out first baseman in Lew Fonseca. Fonseca led the league that year with a .369 batting average and drove in 103 runs. Hauser was used primarily as a pinch hitter.

I had a little stretch when Fonseca got hit in the arm with a ball on the road. I started three games in New York, had six or seven hits in those three games. The Yankee coach told me, "Jesus Christ, Joe, the way you're hitting, Fonseca's gonna get well fast." Grab me?

Hauser won a few games with pinch homers, but when the 1929 season was over, so was Joe's time in the big leagues. It was on to Baltimore in the International League in 1930, and that's where the Joe Hauser legend really began. People talk about you when you hit 63 home runs, and that's how many homers Hauser hit that year. Nobody had ever hit that many home runs in professional baseball before.

Although he again led the league in home runs in 1931, he was hobbling because of a groin injury, and Baltimore sold his contract to the Minneapolis Millers.

JOSEPH "UNSER CHOE" HAUSER

THIS COLORFUL FIRST-BASEMAN WALLOPED 63 HOME RUNS FOR BALTIMORE OF THE INTERNATIONAL LEAGUE IN 1930, AND 69 FOR MINNEAPOLIS OF THE AMERICAN ASSOCIATION IN 1933, TO MERIT THE TITLE OF "HOME RUN KING OF THE MINORS." BORN, JANUARY 12, 1899, AT MILWAUKEE, WISCONSIN. ELECTED IN 1967

Joe Hauser's Wisconsin Athletic Hall of Fame plaque (*Courtesy of the Wisconsin Sports Authority*)

As in Baltimore, the fences in the Minneapolis ballpark were shorter than the fences of most ballparks. The Minneapolis owner, Mike Kelley, had visions of Hauser launching home run after home run in the American Association team's home field, Nicollet Park.

And launch them he did, starting with 49 in 1932. That year he was still getting paid a major league wage. But the next year, his really big year, his salary was cut way back because of the Depression.

The two years I was in Baltimore I got my major league salary, $6,500 a year. And my first year in Minneapolis, in 1932, I got $6,500. The next year I got a contract for $400 a month! They cut me over $600 a month! Jesus Christ. I go and see the boss, wondering if he couldn't pay my rent or something. He said, "No, everybody's getting $400. That's all anybody's getting." Later on, toward the end of the season, I heard he was paying the rent for some of his drunken pitchers.

In 1933 Joe was on a pace to break the home run record he had set two years earlier. During one 21-day stretch he hit 20 homers. The baseballs were flying out of the park. Think of the sound that's made when a slugger connects. You heard that sound all summer long.

Andy Cohen's mother came to town to watch him play. She was with a friend and they got to the park a little late. I was up and I hit a home run. It was a doubleheader, and the first time I got up in the second game I hit another home run. Andy Cohen's mother turned to her friend and said, "Let's go. This is where we came in."

We were playing in Milwaukee one day, I think it was in July, and their pitcher, a fellow named Braxton, says to me, "Joe, I'm going to fix you up today and lay those fastballs right down the guts. Let's see how far you can hit 'em. We ain't going no place, and you've got a hell of a home run record going, and I'm going to see that you hit one off me."

So the game gets started, and he throws a pitch straight at my head. A knockdown pitch. I don't say nothing. I got a base on balls, is how it turned out.

But I know he was worried about me hitting a home run off him. He was working on me with those screwballs that he threw. And his screwball broke into my power, low inside. They were questionable strikes, and if I got ahold of that ball she was a goner.

Now, I remember that game real well. We beat them by one run. Yes, I hit a homer off him. And he was working like hell on me to get me out.

Going into the last week I had 62 home runs. We played a doubleheader on Labor Day. We played a game in St. Paul in the morning—big fence there. I hit two long ones—home runs anywhere. That broke my Baltimore record. It rained that day. There were 10,000 people in the ballpark, and they stopped the game after four innings. If we had five innings in, the game would have been over.

They waited a good hour before they started again. That's when I hit the two homers.

In the afternoon we played another game, in Minneapolis. They used to do that on holidays. The first time up I hit another one. And then I didn't get any more that day. [The impish Hauser explained why he didn't get any more that day: "Because I was tired of hitting home runs."]

That year I hit 69 home runs, drove in 187 runs, and hit something like .340 playing for $400 a month. I started out 1934 with 17 home runs in the month of April. They had me down for a possible 100. But then in June I broke my leg. I was a base runner at first base, and Pinky Hargrave hit a ball into the gap. I was going to score. All I had to do was stay on my feet. I rounded third, and down I went. That was a bad one. My left kneecap was broken in three pieces.

By 1937 I was out of baseball and didn't have a job. Some club in the Coast League offered me a job for $250 a month. Sheboygan knew I was available and they signed me up for $300 a month. So I took that job—only 60 miles from Milwaukee. The Sheboygan Chairmakers, semipro ball. We played about 50 games a year. I played and managed. In 1940 Sheboygan got a team in the Wisconsin State League. I had a real bad ball club in 1940 and 1941. In 1942 we won the pennant. That was my last year as a player. We were out of baseball during the war, 1943, 1944, 1945. In 1946 we played again and we were lucky we didn't finish last. In 1947 we won the pennant. We were affiliated with the Brooklyn Dodgers then. We won pennants in '48 and '51 also. In 1953 the league folded.

Then I managed a team in Tennessee. It was a lousy club, for the Dodgers. Then I managed in Duluth for three years, in the Northern League. We played through the Dakotas. That was my last ball club. It was a good club. We won two pennants.

◆ ◆ ◆

I'm going to be 93 next month. I'm shooting for 100, but it's a long ways. I can't sleep nights—put that in. I hardly get to sleep before four o'clock, but I'm in bed by 11. I'm living alone. My wife died six years ago. I don't go out much. And I don't get any women in here.

Sheboygan manager Joe Hauser, circa 1940 (© *Brace Photo*)

"Joe, maybe they're afraid of you," I said. He replied, *"No, I'm afraid of them!"*

If the phone rings, I don't answer it. Why should I? Nobody owes me any money.

I told Unser Choe I would be speaking to Joe Bauman. Said Hauser, "He's the guy who hit those 72 home runs, isn't he?" I told him he was. "If he'd been in Triple A ball, he'd never hit that many. You know that."

I said I did. I asked Joe if there was anything he'd like me to pass along to Bauman when I talked to him.

"Take a gun along and shoot him," said Hauser with a laugh. Then he added, "There was an umpire who was working in Vero Beach during spring training, and he said he had Bauman in his last game, and Bauman hit three home runs that night. He said the pitchers worked like hell to get him out. They weren't giving him nothing. Three long home runs. They were big jobs."

I was curious if Hauser had thought about returning to the majors when he was tearing up the minor leagues. "I didn't think about it much," he said. "Not after I got through with Cleveland and went to Baltimore. Because I was 31 years old, and they'd say my legs are bad. They wouldn't take a chance on me. So that's what happened. They were scared to take me, afraid it wouldn't be a good deal."

"Say," said Hauser, "did I tell you I was about to turn 93?"

"Joe, I thought it was 103."

"103! When I reach 100," he said, "I'm gonna dig a hole at the cemetery and jump in."

Hauser mentioned that, as a youth, he had pitched for the town team in Waupun, Wisconsin. "There's a prison there. But they never got me in there!"

"You would have busted out," I said.

"Yaaaah."

Joseph (Unser Choe) John Hauser

Born January 12, 1899, Milwaukee, WI. Died July 11, 1997, Sheboygan, WI.
Batted left, threw left. Height: 5' 10½". Weight: 175 lbs.

Year	Club	League	Position	G	AB	R	H	2B	3B	HR	RBI	SB	BA
1918	Providence	Eastern	OF	39	130	17	36	5	6	1	—	4	.277
1919	Providence	Eastern	OF	107	385	64	105	20	21*	6*	—	11	.273
1920	Milwaukee	American Association	OF	156	549	94	156	22	16	15	79	7	.284
1921	Milwaukee	American Association	1B	167	632	126	200	26	9	20	110	12	.316
1922	Philadelphia	American	1B	111	368	61	119	21	5	9	43	1	.323
1923	Philadelphia	American	1B	146	537	93	165	21	10	16	94	6	.307
1924	Philadelphia	American	1B	149	562	97	162	31	8	27	115	7	.288
1925	Philadelphia	American	1B	(did not play; broke leg April 7)									
1926	Philadelphia	American	1B	91	229	31	44	10	0	8	36	1	.192
1927	Kansas City	American Association	1B	169	617	145	218	49	22*	20	134	25	.353
1928	Philadelphia	American	1B	95	300	61	78	19	5	16	59	4	.260
1929	Cleveland	American	1B	37	48	8	12	1	1	3	9	0	.250
1929	Milwaukee	American Association	1B	31	105	18	25	2	0	3	14	2	.238
1930	Baltimore	International	1B	168*	617	173*	193	39	11	63*	175	1	.313
1931	Baltimore	International	1B	144	487	100	126	20	6	31*	98	1	.259
1932	Minneapolis	American Association	1B	149	522	132	158	31	3	49*	129	12	.303
1933	Minneapolis	American Association	1B	153	570	153*	189	35	4	69*	182*	1	.332
1934	Minneapolis	American Association	1B	82	287	81	100	7	3	33	88	1	.348
1935	Minneapolis	American Association	1B	131	409	74	107	18	1	23	101	3	.262
1936	Minneapolis	American Association	1B	125	437	95	117	20	2	34	87	1	.268

Joseph (Unser Choe) John Hauser (*continued*)

Year	Club	League	Position	G	AB	R	H	2B	3B	HR	RBI	SB	BA
1937	Sheboygan	+Wisconsin State	1B	37	131	—	45	12	3	8	38	—	.344
1938	Sheboygan	+Tri-State	1B	49	172	55	55	19	2	10	54	—	.320
1939	Sheboygan	+Tri-State	1B	—	—	—	—	—	—	—	—	—	—
1940	Sheboygan	Wisconsin State	1B	79	204	48	53	16	3	7	32	11	.260
1941	Sheboygan	Wisconsin State	1B	77	233	53	67	13	5	11	54	10	.288
1942	Sheboygan	Wisconsin State	1B	77	242	57	73	17	4	14	70	7	.302
		Major League totals		629	2044	351	580	103	29	79	356	19	.284
		Minor League totals		1854	6426	1430	1923	340	116	399	1353	109	.299
		Combined totals		2473	8470	1781	2503	443	145	478	1709	128	—

+Not affiliated with organized baseball

*Led league

7

ARRESTED FOR PICKPOCKETING

PAUL HINES

A pickpocket was arrested on November 14, 1922, in Washington, D.C. The man, an employee of the Department of Agriculture's post office, was Paul Hines, one of the country's finest turn-of-the-century ballplayers.

This account appeared in the next day's edition of The Washington Star:

Paul A. Hines, 68 years old, and a Washington baseball star of the late eighties, was arrested yesterday afternoon on three charges of pocket-picking.

Hines was taken to police headquarters yesterday afternoon by Detectives James Springman and George Darnall and Policewoman Irene Hubbs, on a charge of having taken Springman's pocketbook from the pocket of Mrs. Hubbs's overcoat at 9th Street and New York Avenue. When he arrived at headquarters two other charges were placed against him.

The gray-haired man has been under surveillance for some time. When his room was searched, at 233 Rhode Island Avenue, a number of purses and pocketbooks were found in it, as well as 25 pairs of eyeglasses and spectacles.

Hines is the last man in Washington the police wanted to arrest on such a charge. His record is known to many of them, and he has many firm friends in the department who did not desert him yesterday in his extremity. His reputation has always been of the highest and Inspector Clifford L. Grant, in charge of the detective bureau, said he was inclined to regard the alleged activities of the man as a kleptomania attendant upon advancing years.

Hines was well-liked and respected in Washington. When he died in 1935, no mention was made in the Washington papers of the arrest. Apparently the pickpocketing habit was thought of as a passing phase and not something for which he should be condemned.

Wrote Guy Smith in *The Sporting News* after Hines's death, "When baseball's *final* pages are written, the name of Paul A. Hines will shine in golden letters. A cleaner, more upright player never set foot on a bag, for he was the type of athlete crowned with all the graces nature can bestow."

Paul Hines was quite a ballplayer, a *fine* hitter, and an excellent *fielder*. And if his name gets added to the Hall of Fame someday, many will nod their heads and say, "It's about time."

Hines was baseball's first Triple Crown winner in 1878, although he led the league with just four home runs. But he did something else that year that baseball historians still write about. Hines made a great catch—a terrific catch—and started one of baseball's most noteworthy triple plays. In a letter published in *The New York Clipper* April 27, 1901, Jack Manning wrote his recollections of the play:

With two men on base—one on second and the other on third—Burdock hit a fly over the shortstop's head, which everybody thought was safe, and both men started for home. [Center fielder] Hines, after a hard run, caught the ball close to the ground and kept on running to third base, putting out the man who had occupied that base before he could return. He (Hines) started for Sutton, who was trying to get back to second base, when somebody shouted to him to throw the ball and he threw to Sweasy, who was playing second base at that time, thereby completing the triple play, which was a dandy, giving Hines two putouts and an assist.

The letter's writer, Jack Manning, was the base runner at third on the play.

Another eyewitness, outfielder Jim O'Rourke, described it like this:

[The play's] effect was electric. . . . I can picture Hines coming down the little slope from center field toward third base with the fleet-footedness of a deer, reaching at full length, catching the ball within an inch of the ground, and not stopping until he landed on third base, from which he returned the ball to second base, thereby completing a triple play, the brilliancy of which I have never seen recalled.

Some of the other eyewitnesses later contended that both base runners had passed third base and that when Hines tagged third he completed an unassisted triple play—quite a feat for an outfielder. Of course it's impossible to know exactly what happened. The story presented by Manning and O'Rourke is the version most widely accepted.

Paul Hines, born in Washington, D.C., on March 1, 1852, began his long baseball career with a team called the Rosedales. He went professional in 1872, with the Washington Nationals of the long-gone National Association. He played first and third. Hines joined the original Chicago White Stockings in 1874. When the National Association disbanded after the 1875 season, Hines remained in Chicago. He was one of the main contributors when the White Stockings won the pennant in 1876, the National League's inaugural year. Then it was on to the Providence Grays, also in the National League, with whom Hines won the batting championship in 1878—although for many years the record books had Hines listed as the runner-up.

As things were, that wasn't such a big deal in those days anyway. What seems to have mattered was who had the most base hits. Today there are the Cy Young and MVP awards, but in the late 1870s the coveted prize was the McKay Medal, which Paul Hines won in 1879 when he slapped out 146 hits, a National League record at that

John J. Burdock

John E. Manning

James O'Rourke

Paul A. Hines

On May 8, 1878, in a game against Boston, Providence outfielder Paul Hines snagged a fly ball hit by John "Blackie" Burdock, starting a dazzling triple play still discussed by baseball historians. Boston second baseman Jack Manning and his teammate, future Hall of Famer James "Orator" O'Rourke, were two eyewitnesses later asked to describe the play, which O'Rourke labeled "phenomenal." (*New York Clipper Woodcuts 1879–1880*) time. Throughout his career Hines had his share of extra-base hits and led the National League in doubles three times.

Overall, Paul Hines played 16 years in the majors—20 if you count his four years in the National Association. When he retired after the 1891 season he had (16-year totals) 1,881 hits, 368 doubles, 1,083 runs scored, and a lifetime batting average of .301. Nine times he batted over .300, with a high mark of .358.

To give a better idea of how Paul Hines was regarded in his day, here's an excerpt from an untitled sheet from the file on Hines at the Baseball Hall of Fame:

> As an outfielder he has but few if any equals, and the wonderful and brilliant running-catches made by him are too numerous to mention in detail. . . . During his entire professional career he has also ranked as one of the best batsmen in the country, standing second in that respect in 1878, and excelling all others during the past season, when he won the elegant gold medal offered by Mr. McKay of Buffalo, N.Y., to the batsman securing the largest number of base hits in League championship games. Hines' batting last season was wonderful, the most noteworthy instance occuring in the concluding championship game between the Providence and Troy Clubs on August 26, when he made six successive safe hits, and also finished the tenth inning and the game in favor of his nine by a magnificent running-catch that left two of the Troys on the bases. In the deciding contest of the League season it was Hines' hard hit after two men were out that sent home the winning run and earned for Providence the right to fly the championship pennant during 1880; and in the memorable eleven-inning game between the Chicagos and Hartfords, on June 19, 1875, it was his hit that scored the only run then made. He is a very quiet and gentlemanly player, and is deservedly popular with all his professional associates.

Paul Hines was the big gun for the Providence Grays from 1878 through 1885 and was the only player who was a member of that team each year of the team's existence. Following his stint with the Grays, Hines played two years in his hometown with the Washington Nationals. According to Guy Smith, Hines was beaned while with Washington by Jim Whitney, which led to at least a partial loss of hearing. This, of course, made things more difficult for him. Guy Smith wrote in 1935 that he had witnessed "Umpires . . . holding up their fingers to indicate balls or strikes to [Hines]. . . ."

Was it because of Paul Hines that umpires started using hand signals to indicate balls or strikes? It's usually said that this practice was begun to help William "Dummy" Hoy, who reached the majors in 1888.

◆ ◆ ◆

This chapter on Paul Hines will end with a semi-jolly clip from his Hall of Fame file. It's dated April 12, 1890, and comes from Pittsburgh:

> PAUL HINES A PITTSBURGHER. Now we have the old reliable hard-hitting Paul Hines with us as a member of the National League Club. He has always been a favorite here, and many of the girls are badly "gone" on his shape. I will never forget the sensation he created here last season when he came on the field one day wearing a shirt that fit him like a kid glove. Paul is by no means an attenuated [scrawny] specimen of mankind, and his appearance in that shirt would have brought a blush to the face of many a fair maid, well accustomed as she might be to the exposure of a decollette costume. In the playing he has done here so far Hines shows he is still as skillful as ever with the stick, and has been hitting the ball hard and often.

So there you have it. Paul Hines: fine hitter, excellent fielder, convicted pickpocket, dashing fellow.

Paul A. Hines

Born March 1, 1852, Washington, D.C. Died July 10, 1935, Hyattsville, MD.
Threw right, batted right. Height: 5' 9". Weight: 173 lbs.

Year	Club	League	Position	G	AB	R	H	2B	3B	HR	RBI	SB	BA
1872	Washington	National Association	1B–3B	11	49	10	14						.286
1873	Washington	National Association	OF–2B–C	39	186	33	61						.328
1874	Chicago	National Association	OF–2B–SS	59	283	47	78						.276
1875	Chicago	National Association	OF–2B	69	322	42	101						.314
1876	Chicago	National	OF–2B	64	305	62	101	21*	3	2	59		.331
1877	Chicago	National	OF–2B	60	261	44	73	11	7	0	23		.280
1878	Providence	National	OF–SS	62	257	42	92	13	4	4*	50*		.358*
1879	Providence	National	OF	85	409*	81	146*	25	10	2	52		.357
1880	Providence	National	OF–2B–1B	85	374	64	115	20	2	3	35		.307
1881	Providence	National	OF–2B–1B	80	361	65	103	27	5	2	31		.285
1882	Providence	National	OF–1B	84	379	73	117	28	10	4			.309
1883	Providence	National	OF–1B	97	442	94	132	32	4	4			.299
1884	Providence	National	OF–1B–P	114	490	94	148	36*	10	3			.302
1885	Providence	National	O–1–2–3–S	98	411	63	111	20	4	1	35		.270
1886	Washington	National	O–3–1–S–2	121	487	80	152	30	8	9	56		.312
1887	Washington	National	O–1–2–S	123	478	83	147	32	5	10	72	46	.308
1888	Indianapolis	National	OF–1B–SS	133	513	84	144	26	3	4	58	31	.281
1889	Indianapolis	National	1B–OF	121	486	77	148	27	1	6	72	34	.305
1890	Pittsburgh & Boston	National	OF–1B	100	394	52	94	13	3	0	57	15	.239
1891	Washington	American Association	OF–1B	54	206	25	58	7	5	0	31	6	.282
	Major League totals—16 years			1481	6253	1083	1881	368	84	56	631	132	.301
	National Association totals—4 years			178	840	132	254						.302
	Combined totals—20 years			1659	7093	1215	2135	368+	84+	56+	631+	132+	.301

*Led league

8

TWENTY-GAME TONY

TONY FREITAS

My ex-girlfriend called me from her home in Sacramento in March of 1994. "I have some bad news," she said. "It's not totally unexpected." I had no idea what she was talking about. "What happened?" She paused and then told me, "Tony Freitas has passed away." I was actually quite surprised. And very upset. Very unhappy.

Freitas was 85 when he died, but he'd been in excellent health. Since many of the players in my book were old, I expected to see some of them pass away eventually, but I thought Freitas would be one of the last to go, not the first. It even crossed my mind that he might eventually become the oldest living former ballplayer—that's how healthy he seemed to be.

I had lived in Sacramento for about 10 years. Every once in a while Bill Conlin would give a little mention to Tony Freitas in his Sacramento Bee *column. At the time I didn't pay much attention. Freitas had played a few years in the majors and many in the minors, winning 342 games, the most ever by a minor league left-hander, but like most baseball fans I hadn't yet awakened to the idea that baseball players didn't need to be big league stars to have something to say.*

Back in September of 1991 I had sent a letter to the Hall of Fame and asked for the year-by-year stats of players I'd heard had interesting minor league careers, and Tony Freitas was one of the players I asked about. When I decided to produce a book on talented but overlooked ballplayers, Tony Freitas was one of the first players I chose to include. His career looked interesting.

I dialed Freitas's number and reached a man who sounded about 50. After he assured me he indeed was the former ballplayer, we talked about my book and he agreed to a future interview. At that time I planned to have other writers write various chapters and I'd enlisted a talented writer named Ed Beitiks to do a profile of Freitas. Since Freitas was amenable, we were all set. I wanted Beitiks because I'd read several articles he'd written for the San Francisco Examiner, *and I could see that besides being a good writer, he cares about people.*

Beitiks drove to Tony Freitas's house for the interview. Freitas later told me, "He gave me quite a grilling. He asked me things I don't think I've ever been asked before." Freitas said he enjoyed the session.

I talked to Tony Freitas several times and got to know him fairly well. He was humble, kind-hearted, and honest. He was a decent man.

Here's the profile Ed Beitiks wrote on the pitcher, who, incidentally, was one of the few Portuguese descendants to reach the major leagues. This chapter was completed before Tony Freitas passed away.

A car pulled up to the green house in Orangevale, northeast of Sacramento, and Tony Freitas walked out of the garage to see who it was. A radio inside was playing "Glow Worm," by the Mills Brothers. Freitas, 84, had a career that spanned 26 years, from the Arizona State League in 1928 to a last game with Stockton of the California League in 1953. The winningest left-hander in minor-league history, with 342 victories, Freitas had nine 20-win seasons and posted a career ERA of 3.11.

While pitching across four decades, Freitas played for the Philadelphia Athletics and the Cincinnati Reds, pitched a no-hitter on his 24th birthday, had a save and a win in the doubleheader that clinched Sacramento's only PCL championship, and—in his final game, on a day when the Stockton club presented him with a brand new car—struck out the last three batters he faced.

Freitas, with his white hair combed back, looked to be the same five-foot-eight and 160 pounds he was in his playing days. He walked inside his house and sat down on a couch to talk about his long playing career, starting with sandlot ball when Warren Harding was in the White House.

Calling back the days of his career, Freitas remembered making it into *Ripley's Believe It or Not* on two occasions, being brought out of jail to pitch a game, playing on 10 different ball clubs, and being a member of a Philadelphia Athletics team that included Jimmie Foxx, Al Simmons, Mickey Cochrane, and Lefty Grove.

He said he taught himself to throw as a youngster, adding that his best pitch was always the curveball. "I never did have what you could call a fastball. For me, it was control, a change-up, the curveball.

"I started throwing the curveball on my own. It came natural, I guess. But the fastball never did come natural."

While playing pickup games in his hometown, Mill Valley, California, Freitas didn't think his arm was good enough to get him anywhere. "I never did know whether I was any good. I just went out there trying to win every ball game I was in. I still say, looking back on it, that I was lucky."

As Freitas was going about his business on the mound, a friend of Sacramento manager Buddy Ryan was watching the youngster. Word got back to Ryan, and before Freitas knew it he'd been invited to Sacramento's spring training in 1928.

Freitas said his father, Antonio, Superintendent of Streets in Mill Valley, "didn't like baseball at first. He told me, 'I'll never let you be a ballplayer.'" But eventually, said Freitas, his father became "baseball crazy."

The Sacramento club assigned Freitas to Phoenix in the Arizona State League his first year, and in 1929 he played for the Globe, Arizona, team for a while, before Sacramento called him up. Freitas had a solid season with Sacramento in 1930, going 19–6. In 1931, he again won 19 games. He received plenty of write-ups for his on-field accomplishments—and for something that happened off the field, in Novato.

"I got quite a few speeding tickets going through there, and the judge said, 'Fining you doesn't do any good. I'm going to put you in jail.'" Freitas, who admitted to "having a heavy foot," especially when he was driving his favorite speedster—a 1929 Model A roadster—was ordered to spend five days in jail.

The Sacramento manager, claiming he was short of pitchers, convinced the judge to release Freitas to pitch a game against the San Francisco Mission Reds.

It was page-one news when Freitas won the game 5–3. He pitched superbly, allowing just two earned runs. He also contributed

Tony Freitas (*Courtesy of James Iovino Jr.*)

two singles and a sacrifice bunt, and registered nine assists. After the game he returned to Novato to finish the remainder of his sentence.

One version of the story has it that a big league scout was in town to see Freitas, and the Sacramento team wanted to showcase its star left-hander in order to make a sale and bring in what would have been a considerable amount of money.

"Some of the players had it in their contracts to get a certain percentage of the sale price," said Freitas, "but it was never in my vocabulary to look for anything like that. I just wanted to go to the big leagues and see what I could do."

Freitas made the big leagues sit up and take notice on May 5, 1932—his 24th birthday—when he pitched a no-hitter against the Oakland Oaks. He was sold to the Athletics soon after and was brought to Philadelphia on the double-quick.

At the time, Connie Mack was quoted as saying, "A southpaw like this comes to baseball only once in 20 years." But his first few outings for the Athletics had Mack swallowing hard. Freitas couldn't get used to being around baseball's best players, he explained. "I was scared stiff, being around all these big league players I'd only read about. To finally be one of them—I was dumbfounded. I was in awe."

Freitas remembered his first big league outing, against the Washington Senators. He was holding onto a one-run lead in the ninth inning when Joe Cronin came to the plate. Mickey Cochrane called time and walked to the mound.

"Cochrane said, 'This guy's a good low-ball hitter—don't throw it down there.' I guess I lost track, though, and threw him a low one. He hit it out and tied the game. We lost in extra innings."

His next start was in Yankee Stadium against Ruth, Gehrig, and the rest of the legendary New York lineup.

"I looked at Ruth at the plate and couldn't believe I was seeing him," he said. But Freitas kept his composure, and when he got two strikes on Ruth he threw him a change-up. Ruth swung and missed. "The fans gave me a big hand and Ruth doffed his cap—doffed his cap to this rookie on the mound.

"I got cocky as the devil. . . . But the next time up he hit one out. That sure deflated me in a hurry." He was further deflated by being saddled with a loss.

"About four or five games in a row there I got shellacked, got the hell knocked out of me. Then I pitched one against Detroit, won it, and went on to win nine more in a row."

Something quite unusual happened during the sixth win of the streak. In the fifth inning there were runners on second and third with one out. Freitas, who always was a good fielder, grabbed a comebacker and saw that the runner was caught a little too far off third. He faked a throw and ran at the runner. He faked a couple more throws, and the runner was stuck leaning, not knowing which way to run. Freitas tagged him. The play happened quickly, and Freitas turned to see where the other runner was. He too was stuck—a little too far off second. Freitas made a fake to second, caught the runner between the bases, and ended up tagging him himself—resulting in an unassisted double play by a pitcher on a ground ball. Freitas was written up in *Ripley's Believe It or Not* for that one.

A year or two earlier, while in the Pacific Coast League, Freitas had made it into *Ripley's Believe It or Not* for another odd and well-executed play. Henry Oana struck out, and the ball got away from the catcher. Freitas rushed in, picked up the ball, and threw out Oana, who wasn't considered slow, at first base.

Freitas finished his rookie season, 1932, with a 12–5 record. It was during the Depression, and Connie Mack, who was having money problems, sent Freitas a contract calling for a $1,400 salary cut.

"I didn't feel so pretty good about that," said Freitas. "I thought I should have been offered a raise, not a cut. He [Mack] said, 'We've got too many high-priced ballplayers on the club as it is.' And I was saying to myself, 'So why take it out on the little potato, the little kid, the rookie?'" In the end, Freitas signed his 1933 contract for the same amount of money he had received the previous year.

After his feast-or-famine first year in the majors, Freitas returned to the Athletics in 1933 and "got off to a lousy start, got a little arm trouble." He was sent to Portland, where he finished out the season at 4–7, trying to figure out what had changed.

"If I knew what I was doing wrong, I never would have lost another ball game," he explained. "But there are things you just can't figure out. When you do something right, you ask yourself, 'What causes it?' Well, I don't have an answer."

Freitas started out 1934 at St. Paul and moved on to Cincinnati in the National League. "I have a lot of good memories out of Cincinnati," said Freitas. One reason, he explained, was that he had more friends on the team, players he had known in the Pacific Coast League.

Tony Freitas was on hand in Cincinnati on May 23, 1935, when the first major league night game was played. Said Freitas, "President Roosevelt pressed a button in Washington and lit the lights in

While pitching for Cincinnati, Tony Freitas once dueled Dizzy Dean for 17 innings. (© *Brace Photo*)

Crosley Field." Freitas had also been part of the first night game in PCL history, five years earlier, in Sacramento.

One of Tony Freitas's most memorable outings occured in Cincinnati on a very hot July afternoon. The opposing team was St. Louis, and the Cardinals' pitcher was Dizzy Dean.

"I'll never forget that game," said Freitas. "We'd get a couple of runs and they'd get a couple of runs, and the game stayed tied for 17 innings. I lost nine pounds that day. And I didn't have nine pounds to lose.

"Charlie Dressen finally took me out in the 17th inning, for a pinch hitter, and then they took Diz out. But he still won the game. It went 18 innings. That was in 1934, the year Dean won 30 games."

The radio was playing "The Naughty Lady of Shady Lane" as Tony Freitas looked past the sliding glass doors to the patio and backyard. "The biggest difference between the big leagues now and then is that we were just a bunch of kids, really," he said. "Now, there's so much more money involved, the players can't take it easy. There's too much pressure on them."

Back then he heard stories of camp followers and baseball groupies, "but I never had any follow me. I wasn't looking. I don't know much about that kind of merchandise." What he ended up doing when the team pulled into town, Freitas explained, was go window-shopping. "I used to walk the streets, go window-shopping, all day long."

Teammates would come around with cold beers. "I never did acquire a taste for beer," he said. "I'm a Pepsi boy."

The Pepsi boy had losing seasons in 1934 and 1935. In 1936, he started out with an 0–2 record and was sold to Columbus. The Cardinals owned the Columbus team as well as the team in Sacramento. On his way to Columbus, Freitas stopped in St. Louis to see Branch Rickey.

"It was my wife's idea to talk to Mr. Rickey," said Freitas. "Sacramento and Columbus were both in the same classification, and I would much rather play in Sacramento, which was in my backyard.

"Mr. Rickey said he would see what he could do, and after the season, the Columbus team sold me to Sacramento." Back in California, Freitas really settled in, reeling off one 20-game season after another.

As before, he relied on a good curveball and excellent control, but he worked on developing his screwball. "I think that helped me quite a bit," he said. "I used it whenever I was in a jam."

"After I came back to Sacramento, after I had two 20-game seasons, Mr. Rickey came out. He got me aside and he said, 'Tony, I'm here to see about making a deal for you, to bring you back to the big leagues.'

"I said, 'Mr. Rickey, if it's all the same to you, I would just as soon finish my career in the Pacific Coast League.' I told him, 'I had a chance to pitch in the American League, and I had a chance in the

National League, and I don't feel good back there. And I feel great out here.' . . . And I had better luck out here.

"He said, 'Then this is where you'll stay.' And that was it."

Freitas doesn't second-guess his short major league career. "Sometimes you're just not good enough to stay up there in the big leagues. It's pretty simple, really. If you win, you stay. If you lose, so long."

Things were more low-key in the PCL, said Freitas. Players were loose, pulling pranks every chance they got. "You'd always find someone who'd nail a glove down to a seat or put somebody else's mail up on the ceiling."

Freitas wasn't above having some fun himself. He'd buy leftover army-store dynamite, roll it into homemade firecrackers, and toss them out on the field from time to time.

The biggest difference between the PCL and the majors, said Freitas, was that "each player was a little bit better in the majors. You got a good pitcher out there every day, instead of once or twice a week. And everybody in the lineup could hit, where in the Coast League you'd have some gaps."

Freitas said he pitched to "get out the bad hitters. The good ones were going to get their hits. What you didn't want to do was put the bad hitters on so the good ones could drive them in."

There were usually seven games a week in the PCL, with a day off Monday and a doubleheader on Sunday. Freitas remembered the long train trips to Seattle to get to Rainier Field, where "you'd sit in the dugout—it was below the ground—and see the outfielders from just the waist up."

Other forgotten PCL ballparks came to mind. The Oaks' home field in Emeryville. Seals Stadium. Recreation Park in San Francisco. Gilmore Field in Hollywood. Wrigley Field in Los Angeles, with its wraparound, wooden stands—"as good a ballpark as you could look at." And there was Moreing Field—later Edmonds Field—in Sacramento. "I used to love to pitch there," said Freitas.

Freitas remembered the end of the 1942 season, when Sacramento won its only PCL championship. "Los Angeles came into Sacramento with a two-game lead, with one series to go—seven games. They beat me the first game, which made them three games out in front. And then they beat Blix Donnelly—that put them four games out in front, with five games to go, and then we won the next five in a row."

The last two wins were a doubleheader sweep. With over 11,000 people watching, Sacramento came back from a 5–0 deficit in the first game to go ahead 7–5 in the ninth. In the bottom of the ninth, Tony Freitas came out of the bull pen and retired the side, one-two-three.

After that, manager Pepper Martin was squinting at his lineup card, trying to decide which of his pitchers would get the call for the second game. Recalled Freitas, "Pepper looked around and said, 'Who am I going to pitch now?' and I said, 'Well, I'm hot. Why don't I pitch it?'"

Freitas did, winning 5–1 on a four-hitter, and making a name for himself in Sacramento for as long as baseball is played.

Said Freitas, "Those people in Sacramento, they went crazy. People were all over the outfield, all around the plate. That field got crowded."

As the Pacific Coast memories came back to Freitas, so did the names. "Bill Schuster played shortstop for Los Angeles, and he was a bit of a comic. He'd fly out to end an inning, but you'd see him race around to second or third and slide into the bag."

And there was Bud Beasley. "Bud really put on quite a show for the people. He'd go through all kinds of different windups, windups that weren't normal for a pitcher." And Freitas mentioned how Beasley would punch holes in his glove and fill the holes with talcum powder. He'd slam the glove with his hands to create a cloud of dust around him, and then he'd pitch out of the middle of the cloud.

Freitas ran down a list of other PCL names:

- Oscar "Ox" Eckhardt: "He was the most unorthodox hitter I ever saw. He was a left-handed hitter, but he *couldn't* hit the ball to right. He hit all those line drives to left. They played him over there and he *still* hit the ball between them. He was quite a hitter."
- Henry "Prince" Oana: "He had a real good future in front of him. He had all the tools. He could run. He had a good arm— he could throw real good. And he had pretty good power."

- Sam Gibson: "Sad Sam of the San Francisco Seals. A real good competitor."
- Dick Barrett: "Kewpie Dick Barrett. I don't know why they called him Kewpie, unless it was that roly-poly face of his. He was quite a competitor, too—do anything to win, and you can't condemn a man for that."
- Ike Boone: "Left-handed hitter. Real good power hitter."
- Joe Marty: "Great ballplayer. All the tools in the world to be a hero of the ballparks. He could run, hit, throw."
- Lefty O'Doul: "As a manager he was real congenial, loved to talk. And he was a good man, a real good man, for the game of baseball."
- Nick Cullop: "A power hitter. An outdoorsman, loved hunting and fishing. My kind of man."
- Jigger Statz: "One heck of an outfielder."
- Joe Sprinz: "Helluva catcher. I saw him at Joe Orengo's funeral four, five years ago."

◆ ◆ ◆

After the 1942 season, Freitas joined the military and didn't play ball again, professionally, until 1946.

"I never did get back to form," said Freitas. He was still a fairly effective pitcher, but the 20-win seasons in the PCL were over. Before he went in the service, he had won 20 or more games six years in a row.

In 1948, when Freitas was 40 years old, his ERA was a very decent 3.09, but he had dropped to 12 wins, and in 1949, he won only four ball games. Freitas explained that the aging process was diminishing his effectiveness as a pitcher. "You lose the elasticity, the flexibility out of your arm. The curve wouldn't break as sharply; the fastball wouldn't be as good. Even your control is affected by it. So everything works against you, as you get older."

If you think Tony Freitas was crushed when Sacramento released him in 1950, think again. This is the Pepsi boy, the guy who exploded firecrackers to keep his teammates loose, the man who won ravioli-eating contests and entertained fans and friends with his cheerful accordion playing.

Tony Freitas knew about thinking positively, and he still wanted to play ball. "I really enjoyed playing. I wasn't ready to quit."

Sacramento held a night for Freitas and retired his number, 17, but they had to make arrangements with the Modesto club so that he could attend the night in his honor. Freitas had hooked on with the Modesto Reds in the California League, a couple of notches below the Pacific Coast League. Freitas went on to win 20 games for Modesto in 1950 while leading the league with an ERA of 2.56. He was the leading pitcher in the California League in 1951, with 25 victories, and in 1952, he switched over to the Stockton club, a little closer to home, and had another fine season.

The radio was playing "Three Coins in the Fountain," as Freitas talked about the latter part of his career. "I told my wife in 1952 that this was going to be my last year. But I won 18 games for Stockton and I said, 'Damn, I could do this another year.' The next year I won 22 and they gave me a new car in my last game.

"It was a 1953 Ford and they drove it out to the mound. I drove it off the mound, came back, and pitched a great game. Usually, you have a bad game when people make a big thing of something. But I threw a shutout. I had a real lucky streak going."

Freitas was 45 years old when he stepped off the mound, having whiffed the final three batters he faced. "A lot of great things happened in my career, but that was the greatest, that last year," he said.

The man of the hour and the decade, Freitas could have lived without the next two years. He became a coach with Sacramento and then was talked into managing the team, leading the Solons to a 76–96 record and a last place finish in 1955.

"It was the biggest mistake I ever made," he said. "I just don't have the personality to be a manager. They wanted you to chew out your players in front of everybody and I didn't like that. I just couldn't do that.

"I got fired, and that was the end of my baseball career." Freitas left the game, went to work as a mechanic for Aerojet, and then retired after 14 years. He grinned, saying, "That's the best job I ever had—Retired."

◆　◆　◆

Nowadays, Freitas will get together with another old player, a player like Wally Westlake, and head for a nearby river or lake for a day's worth of fishing. "We'll sit out there in the boat for six, seven hours, just talking baseball," said Freitas.

Even now, almost 40 years after he last put on a uniform, people come up to Freitas when he's in a grocery store or on the street. "They say, 'It's nice to see you,' and start talking about the time I did one thing or the other."

The radio was playing "Because of You," and Freitas smiled again. "Baseball has been my life," he said, "and I'm still crazy about it. I still see as many games as I can, every summer, on TV.

"If I had it all to do over again, I'd do the same thing," he said. "I still say that I didn't have all that much going for me. I was just lucky, is all."

He laughed to himself and fingered an old clipping from a scrapbook on the coffee table, remembering what it felt like to come out of Mill Valley as a 20-year-old pitcher—a glove tucked under one arm and a long, satisfying baseball career slowly unfolding in front of him.

Antonio (Tony) Freitas

Born May 5, 1908, Mill Valley, CA. Died March 13, 1994, Orangevale, CA.
Batted right, threw left. Height: 5' 8". Weight 161 lbs.

Year	Club	League	G	IP	W	L	R	H	ER	SO	BB	ERA
1928	Phoenix	Arizona State	14	116	5	4	70	116	59	36	27	4.58
1929	Globe	Arizona State	28	167	12	11	104	190	67	104	47	3.61
	Sacramento	Pacific Coast	18	59	2	4	48	73	42	27	29	6.41
1930	Sacramento	Pacific Coast	42	275	19	6	116	287	99	121	74	3.24
1931	Sacramento	Pacific Coast	39	297	19	13	128	311	102	156	102	3.09
1932	Sacramento	Pacific Coast	11	65	6	4	33	53	26	35	28	3.61
1933	Philadelphia	American	23	150	12	5	68	150	64	31	48	3.83
	Philadelphia	American	19	64	2	4	56	90	52	15	24	7.27
	Portland	Pacific Coast	11	75	4	7	44	102	33	48	15	3.98
1934	St. Paul	American Association	8	46	2	3	17	38	16	17	8	3.13
	Cincinnati	National	30	153	6	12	80	194	68	37	25	4.01
1935	Cincinnati	National	31	144	5	10	95	174	73	51	38	4.57
1936	Cincinnati	National	4	7	0	2	2	6	1	1	2	1.29
	Columbus	American Association	25	126	10	8	94	170	82	49	30	5.86
1937	Sacramento	Pacific Coast	37	290	23	12	103	262	92	108	36	2.86
1938	Sacramento	Pacific Coast	38	290	24	11	103	298	86	159	46	2.67
1939	Sacramento	Pacific Coast	43	332*	21	18*	130	350	106	172*	37	2.87
1940	Sacramento	Pacific Coast	41	332*	20	19	128	350*	100	146	48	2.71
1941	Sacramento	Pacific Coast	41	300	21	15	101	297	90	112	38	2.70
1942	Sacramento	Pacific Coast	44	295	24	13	108	322	96	98	36	2.93
1943–45	(military service)											

1946	Sacramento	Pacific Coast	40	296	16	20	104	307	77	126	50	2.34
1947	Sacramento	Pacific Coast	41	215	13	17	103	242	92	104	46	3.85
1948	Sacramento	Pacific Coast	31	192	12	11	81	221	66	59	32	3.09
1949	Sacramento	Pacific Coast	31	78	4	4	38	88	35	31	26	4.04
1950	Sacramento	Pacific Coast	9	11	0	1	11	14	11	4	12	9.00
	Modesto	California	33	218	20	6	84	198	62	134	37	2.56*
1951	Modesto	California	41	283	25*	9	119	277	94	153	43	2.99
1952	Stockton	California	36	268	18	13	106	263	87	151	40	2.92
1953	Stockton	California	34	279*	22*	9	100	261	74	174	45	2.38
	Major League totals		107	518	25	33	301	614	258	135	137	4.48
	Minor League totals		736	4905	342	238	2073	5090	1694	2324	932	3.11

Led league

9

SEVENTY-TWO HOMERS
IN A SEASON

JOE BAUMAN

I used to think of Joe Bauman as sort of a cartoon character, a mythical slugger who banged out prodigious home runs in games played in Southwest towns that can't be found on any map. Was there really a Joe Bauman? Did he really play for a team called the Roswell Rockets in a league called the Longhorn League? Did he really hit 72 home runs in 1954? I know he did, but there's always been something unreal about it.

After looking at Joe Bauman's complete stats, year by year, it finally got through to me that Bauman was an actual flesh-and-blood human, just like the rest of us (but still he remains the only person on earth able to say he reached the 70 home-run mark during baseball's first 127 years of league play).

The more I thought about him the more I knew I wanted to interview him. There were questions. Why did he miss the 1949–51 seasons? What has it been like for him to have hit more home runs than anyone else? Did he ever have dreams of making the major leagues? I also thought he could give me (and my readers) an idea of what it was like playing baseball in the low minors in the 1940s and '50s.

I called directory assistance for the area of Oklahoma where Bauman was born but found nothing. Ballplayers often end up living where they played, so I tried Roswell, New Mexico. He was listed.

I tried to reach him a few weeks later, but the experience wasn't a good one. A woman answered the phone. She barked something about being "tired of this stuff" and hung up. Apparently they didn't want to talk about baseball.

Was it his wife? His daughter? A wrong number? I kept doing my research and in a few weeks called again. Again the phone was slammed in my ear.

I'm thin-skinned by nature and have trouble with rejection, but I eventually tried once more. This time the woman, who I later learned was Bauman's wife Dorothy, was as sweet as could be and put me through to the legend.

It turns out they'd been getting crank phone calls—it had nothing to do with baseball—and their nerves were a little frayed.

I told Joe I wanted to know what he was thinking as his career progressed and what he was feeling along the way. He couldn't have been more accommodating. I'm amazed at how lucky I've been. Like most of the players I've talked with, Joe Bauman was open and articulate and had plenty to say.

This chapter is a bit of a hybrid—a cross between a first-person account and an interview. I left some of the questions in at the middle and end of the chapter to show the forthrightness of Joe's answers.

JOE BAUMAN: My dad worked for Railway Express Company, which is defunct now, and he was transferred to Oklahoma City when I was one year old. And that's where I grew up.

We lived right next to the school yard, and neigborhood kids, we'd get out there and play baseball all the time, after school and everything else. I played every chance I could when I was a kid.

I was always kind of tall for my age. Tall and awkward. I played three sports in high school—football and basketball and baseball too, of course. I loved baseball. The other two I just played because they expected me to. The final year in high school I done pretty good and got on an American Legion team. We won the state championship and things kind of took off from there.

Old Bert Niehoff lived in Oklahoma City, and he was the manager of the Little Rock club, and I signed with him. I had other offers, but I went with Little Rock, which was an independent team. They made their living developing players and selling them to big league clubs.

Little Rock was a Double A team, in the Southern Association, along with Atlanta and New Orleans, Nashville, Knoxville—those teams. So right out of high school, as soon as I graduated, I got on a train and headed down there.

I stayed in Little Rock two or three days—it wasn't the plan for me to make that team right out of high school—and then they sent me out to Newport, Arkansas, to get some seasoning.

My mother died, right in the middle of the damn year, and I took off and went home, and it was just kind of a bad year. It kind of hit me pretty hard, and the war broke out. That was in '41, my first year of playing.

I wasn't eligible for the draft. I wasn't old enough. But I went to work in an aircraft factory in Wichita, Kansas. Beechcraft plant. They had a couple of baseball teams, and I played there that year, and the next year I was in the Navy. I was stationed at Norman, Oklahoma, right off the south edge of the University of Oklahoma. I was there three and a half years.

It was one of those bases where they gathered athletes. Charley Gelbert, the old St. Louis Cardinal shortstop, was head of the athletic department. And there was a captain who was a sport nut too, and they gathered these athletes. There were basketball players, boxers, and baseball was his favorite. They wanted a good baseball team, and they ended up getting one.

I went up and saw Mr. Gelbert and told him my experience, and he had me come out, and damned if he didn't keep me on to play, and most of the guys I was playing with were either major leaguers or American Association, International League type players.

It was a training school, for aviation mates, ordnance men, first one thing and then the other. My job was in the athletic department—calisthenics. As long as the men were in school, it was the policy they'd take their calisthenics. I hated the Navy, but I was damn fortunate to have it work out the way it did. It could have been a lot worse.

"Why'd you hate the Navy?" I asked.

I just didn't like the regimentation of it, any of that military stuff. When I turned 19 I knew my draft number was coming up, and I knew it was down the line, and I just figured, well, hell, if I'm going to have to go I'll just go down and beat them to the punch and join the Navy. I think I'd rather be in the Navy on one of those ships than I would in some trench some place.

When the war ended I still belonged to Little Rock, and as soon as I got out I went back to Little Rock and, my god, I never saw so many ballplayers in my life. They just built up during the war and then all of them were released. Little Rock I'll bet you had 125 ballplayers in spring training. And they sent me, farmed me out to Amarillo, in the West Texas League, and I played there in '46.

I went back to Little Rock in the spring of '47, and they wanted to send me to Jackson, Mississippi, and I told the owner, I said, "Man, for three and a half years I played with better ballplayers than you've got here in Little Rock and made their ball club and everything, and I think I'm ready to move up a notch or two."

He said, "We think you need maybe a little more seasoning."

Well, he could have been right, as far as that was concerned. Anyway, I told him I wasn't going to Jackson. If I went anywhere I'd just go back to Amarillo. I had played there and I enjoyed it that one year. There wasn't any use in going down in all those mosquitoes in Jackson, Mississippi.

He said, "We've got a deal for you to go down to Jackson."

"Well, I'm not going."

Back in those days you didn't have any choice. You either played or you quit. There wasn't any freedom. A club owned you as long as they wanted to. I just told him, "Well, I'll go on home to Oklahoma City. I'll see you later." And I just walked out.

So, anyway, I took off and went home, and I was home about two weeks—I wasn't even there that long—about a week, and they called me and told me to go on and report to Amarillo. Which I did. I'd had a good year in Amarillo in '46. So I just went back to Amarillo and had a little better year—not quite as many home runs but a better batting average. That was one thing they told me. They said that I needed to bring up my average a bit.

In '46 I set the league record in home runs, 48. And the next year I concentrated on keeping my average up real good, which I did.

That winter they sold me to the Boston Braves. And Boston assigned me to Milwaukee, in the American Association. Milwaukee had won the American Association title the year before, and a guy named Heinz Becker was playing first base. He had won the batting title. When I got there I didn't much figure that I'd make that team. But anyway, I stayed with them through spring training and the first few days of the season, and then they sent me to Hartford.

And I got down there, and there's a guy named Ray Sanders, first baseman. They had acquired him from St. Louis. He was fielding, receiving a throw at first base. The throw was a little wide, into the runner coming down, and he was a right-handed first baseman. He stuck out his arm to tag the runner, and he just snapped the bone in his arm. Broke his arm.

So after he healed, they took Ray to spring training, and he hadn't come around well enough to suit them, so they shipped him down to Hartford, where I was. And that put me on the damn bench again. Pinch-hitting and, oh, I played, not many games. We'd more or less alternate.

I looked at the stats. "I can see that. 98 games and 276 at bats. That looks like a lot of pinch hitting."

It was. I pinch-hit a lot, and he would pinch-hit when I played. And it just wasn't too good a year. For me it wasn't. So the next year they sent me a contract and wanted to cut my salary. Hell, all I was making was a damn living anyway.

Back in those days, oh, you'd make—in fact, I'll just tell you. I had a contract for $600 a month, and they wanted to cut the damn thing to about four. And I just told them, hell no. I told the general manager at Hartford.

Money—the incentive of huge money—was not in baseball in those days. What you could do was just figure on every year making a living and trying to save a little bit. And I did. I'd always go back and I'd get me a job during the winter and try to save what I'd accumulated in the summer.

But you just fought them every year for the damn salary. It didn't make any difference where you were playing, whether it's Amarillo or Hartford or Milwaukee. There wasn't that much difference in the salaries. And even if you made it to the big leagues, for a few years all you made was a living, unless you turned into a Ted Williams or something like that, and even they didn't do so good until the tail end of their career. But that's the backdrop you're playing in during those days. You fought them every year for all you could get.

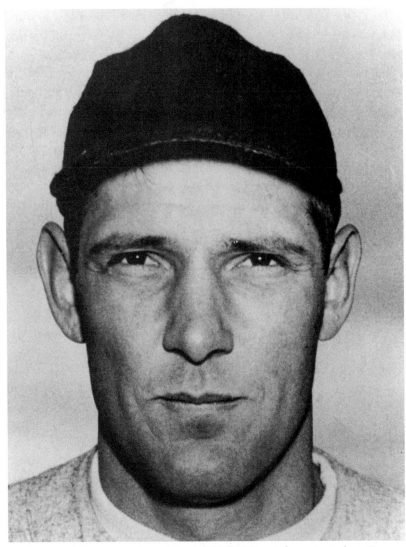

Joe Bauman (*Courtesy of National Baseball Hall of Fame Library & Archive, Coopers-town, NY*)

So they wanted to cut me from about $600 to about $400, and I told the general manager—I tell ya, I didn't like him anyway—and I just said, "No, I'm not gonna do that, at all." I told him, "I can make more money than that peddling 24-inch shoestrings on the corner."

He said, "Take it or leave it."

"Well, I'm leaving it." So I just stayed in Oklahoma City.

Oklahoma and Texas and those places, back then, they had these semipro teams. They would pay you or get you a job or something, and you'd play baseball three or four days a week. Or sometimes five days a week for their town team.

Well, Elk City, Oklahoma, had an oil boom about then, and they were flush with money. And they got the notion that they wanted a top-notch semipro team. They went to gathering their players up, and a bunch of them I knew, and the manager came to Oklahoma City to talk to me. He wanted me to come out there and play, and he told me their ultimate goal was to go to Wichita and try to win that national semipro tournament they have there. Well, I hadn't heard from Boston, so I told him yeah, I'd go, if he'd pay me enough to live on. And damn if he didn't pay me what they wouldn't at Boston.

He said, "Just come on out there, and hell, you won't have to play but three or four games a week and go fishing the rest of the time." And so I did.

He said, "Will you stay then?" 'Cause he wanted to get this team set, and I said, "If I tell you I will, I will."

So I went out there. I was out there about two weeks—we were just kind of training, getting ready to go—and damn if I didn't get a call from Boston. They wanted me to report. They asked me— they didn't tell me, they asked me this time—if I'd report to Atlanta, down in the Southern Association.

They needed a first baseman, and I told them, "Hell no." I said, "You should have spoke up some time ago. I've already given these people my word and I'm going to stay down here and play this summer."

Well, anyway, I played there—three years. Until their oil boom kind of dried up, and their wallets did too. They couldn't afford that ball club anymore, and they disbanded the thing. But we did, we went off to that national tournament all three years. We went into the finals one year undefeated. Finished second or third.

"Were you still thinking about going further on, in baseball, at that point?" I asked.

I'd kind of given up on it at that time, on account of my age. After those four years, you might say, in the service, and then laying out those three years there, why, hell, I was getting up to 27, 28 years old, and I knew the time clock was running out on me. And, oh, you'd like to have gone off to the big leagues, but again, I want to emphasize that the money was not there, even in the big leagues. The motivation would have been, the idea of playing there. The notoriety, or ego, or whatever you want to say.

"Was there ever a point when you thought maybe you didn't have the ability, or there was something that would have held you back?"

Well, you don't know, and that's always a possibility—or a fact. But you don't know it. And I know, during the war, we played on that team. I was pretty young, 19, 20, and 21 years old. We faced big league pitchers, and I held my own. I wasn't the outstanding star on that team or anything, but I made the damn ball club, and they didn't ship me out to the South Pacific. I really don't know. You wonder sometimes whether you could do it or not. But I never truthfully had the opportunity to get on a ball club where they said, "Well, you're the first baseman 'til you prove you can't handle it." In those higher leagues it was just a pinch-hit role or, "Go in and play these last few innings," something like that. You never got the feel of the thing. Never got your feet on the ground. Or, at least, I never did.

"It wasn't like a certain type of pitcher gave you a lot of trouble, like a lefty that threw a good curveball, or . . ."

Oh, in the latter part of my years, left-handers didn't bother me, up until maybe the last two or three years I played. You're playing down there in these damn low minors and they're wilder than hell anyway. [Laughs.] They throw hard, and you don't know where they're throwing, and they don't either. Damn, I've seen some of these kids down here in these minor leagues that could throw a damn marshmallow through a brick wall.

I kind of like the remark Musial made one time. He "didn't particularly like to hit off left-handers." He "just tolerated them." I never did know of a left-handed hitter who liked to hit off a left-handed pitcher. I don't care what they say.

◆ ◆ ◆

I bought me a Texaco service station with another ballplayer when I first went up to Elk City. That was my job, plus playing ball, so it would make it a little more lucrative.

After that third year, there in Elk City, there was a doctor who came by, came in and stopped at the station there and introduced himself. I didn't know who he was, but he had heard of me.

He was from Artesia, New Mexico. He said, "Say, I'm going to the minor league meeting," and was telling me about Artesia and this ball club, and he said, "Would you come out there and play if I bought your contract from Boston?"

I said, "Well, I don't know. We need to talk about this." I said, "If you give any more than a jockstrap for it you're a damn fool."

He said, "Well, I may try to get it. I'd like to know if you'd come play."

I said, "Depends on what the deal is." I knew baseball was playing out in Elk City.

He went off to the winter meeting and came back through there and said, "Well, I bought your contract." He never did tell me what he gave up for it. I didn't ask.

He was a big-money supporter of the Artesia team. And he liked baseball. He made me a hell of a deal, paid me the money I wanted to go there, and he said, "If you don't like it, after you play one year I'll just hand you your outright release. You can go anywhere you want." Well, that was a lucrative deal for me. I mean, I liked that part of it.

I went out there and played and enjoyed the summer. That winter I made a deal with my partner in the service station in Elk City, and he bought me out, and I moved to Artesia.

Artesia was an independent team. But after the second year they got a working agreement with Dallas, out in the Texas League, and Dallas was gonna send them a complete team. So they didn't need me anymore.

So I exercised my right and took my release, and I came up here to Roswell and signed on with them. I got me a little bonus to sign and a good salary and everything else, and I played here that year. That was in 1954.

When I first got up here I bought me a brand-new Texaco station. I kind of hit it lucky. So I was in business here. Worked in the daytime and played ball at night.

That went on for three years: '54, '55, and really, at that stage of the game, I was trying to find some place to settle down and get the hell out of it. It was more or less a dead end, far as that's concerned, and I was at the age I wasn't going anywhere. I really actually played a year longer than I intended to. I intended to play a couple of years, get my service station established, and quit. They talked me into playing that third year, which I really didn't want to do.

"You were hurt that year, right?"

Yeah. My wife and I had built us a new house out here, and that winter we had a hell of a snowstorm, which we don't usually have in this part of the country—but we did that winter. And it snowed clear up on the front porch. You couldn't tell where the steps were or anything. And going to the service station one morning, I went out and stepped off the porch and hit the edge of the step and just went tumbling. I hollered to my wife, "Come out here and help me up. I can't get up." So she did and I got inside.

I hurt my ankle pretty bad, and the doctor x-rayed it. He said, "It's just a bad sprain." But he said, "You've got a bunch of bone chips in there that really should be cut into and got out of there, because in later years they may give you some trouble."

I told him, "No, I don't want to do that." He went ahead and treated it—sprained ankle—and I got over it.

But the next year it got where it hurt me to run. My ankle would hurt. Walking or anything like that didn't bother me. But starting, quick, the pain would shoot up. So about the middle of that year I checked with them about quitting. It was a good excuse anyway. I told them, "I've had it. My ankle's hurting, I can't hardly move around. I'm gonna quit." And that's the way it went.

If I had it to do over, you know, you're young, foolish, but if I had it to do over again I would of had a little different attitude. I would have gone ahead, with Boston, and done whatever they wanted. If they wanted to send me to Timbuktu and pay me $150 a month, if I could have lived on it, why, I would have done it. I should have done it. And played out the string to the point where I could see that I wasn't going to get up, wasn't going to make it. But I guess I was just independent enough and young enough. Didn't have good counsel on that. Had to be my own counsel. But I just couldn't put up with what they were trying to do to me and were doing to me.

Back then they wouldn't advance you too much a year, even though you were having pretty good years. I've talked to other ballplayers that went through it. They'd increase you just enough to get you back, kinda halfway keep you happy.

"It sounds to me if you'd gone with Boston, gone for that $400 a month, you wouldn't have been happy."

I know that. I knew that. I wasn't going forward. I was going backward with them. That's the feeling I had. And if they had called me, well, I had already given my word to that semipro outfit at Elk City.

"You've got to feel good about that."

I do. And I really enjoyed those three years.

"What do you think about all those home runs you were hitting?"

I was a late developer, I guess you would call it, as far as having any power was concerned. Well, the first sign of it was at Amarillo, my first year I played there. I hit 48 that year.

"I know that was the most in baseball that year."

Well, I don't know. It might have been. But it broke the record that existed there (in the West Texas–New Mexico League). And I got to feel, "Well, maybe I am, you know, maybe I can hit home runs." Well, let's see, at that time I was about 24. And the next year I hit, I don't know, 30-something odd home runs.

"How about later on, when you were hitting 50, 53, and 72? What was that like for you, when you were hitting so many home runs?"

Well, it was enjoyable! [Laughs.] They got a habit out here, in this—well, I'd never run into it until I went to Amarillo—where if you hit a home run they'd stick a damn dollar bill through that chicken wire. And you'd go around—they'd expect you to go around—and pick them up. The fans would. And that got to be kind of lucrative.

Hell, it was right after the war, and people had bags full of money. There wasn't anything they could spend it on during the war, and they just saved. Everybody had plenty of money. And, oh, they'd poke that money in that chicken wire, and the ballpark was full every night.

That was before television. They didn't have anything else to do, and they'd come out to the ballpark. There wasn't hardly a night that went by in Amarillo, unless it rained or something, where they weren't sold out. And if you hit a home run, depending on the game situation, you could pick up some pretty good money.

"So if it's a home run in the second inning you get a little bit; you hit a grand slam in the ninth . . ."

Well, a little bit there in Amarillo was, I'd say, a hundred. If you hit a game winner, or something like that, in the eighth or ninth inning, it worked out pretty well.

The first one I hit there in Amarillo—well, I joined them a little late, after spring training—and the first night there I hit a damn home run. I just came on around and went in the dugout. A guy said, "Joe, go up there and get that money!"

"What are you talking about?" I didn't know what he was talking about. Nobody else had hit a home run that game where I could see what would happen. And I looked up there and that money poked through there looked like Bermuda grass. It didn't take me long to learn. [Laughs.]

There was a guy there got married at home plate. He was a pitcher. There was so many people there in that ballpark that they had to rope it off. They were around the outfield, several deep, and if the ball went into them, it was a ground-rule double.

They were clear out to the foul lines, down the foul lines, and the stands were full. And damn if this guy, this pitcher, about the seventh or eighth inning, he hit a home run. The guy who'd got married at home plate. They had to hold that game up—oh, I don't know, it was 30, 45 minutes. Until they went around and gathered that money up. It was the damnedest thing.

There was about a bushel and a half of money. It wasn't all ones, either. There were fives, tens in there and everything else. In fact the ballplayers went trying to help him gather it up. They finally went and got a basket and started putting it in there. The visiting club even went down their side, over there, and gathered the money up and brought it over. They wanted to get the game going. I never saw so much loose money like that. I'll bet there was a bushel and a half of it.

"Do you mind talking a little about 1954? What was that like?"

It was just one of those years. I don't know what caused that year. To be frank with you, it just, I had to be at my peak, in my prime, as far as ability was concerned, that particular year. And I never had any colds or wasn't hurt that year at all. I can't explain it. I wish I could. To hit that many.

Joe Bauman blasting one of his record-setting 72 home runs in 1954. (*Courtesy of the Historical Society for Southeast New Mexico*)

"That number looks pretty strange on paper—72 home runs. All those numbers look strange: 224 RBIs."

Yeah, it is.

"I did some math, and I looked at other great years that people had, and you by far had the highest percentage of home runs for at bats. And lifetime you have the highest percentage too. Did you know that?"

No, I didn't.

"For lifetime, you hit home runs more often than anybody. And that includes Sadaharu Oh. I checked his figures too."

Oh yeah. The Japanese guy.

"I know I'm coming back to this, and you're probably tired of it."

No, no.

"But in '54, what was happening with the fans and the press and all that?"

Oh, they . . . Of course, down on the tail end of it, you know the record had been there quite a while: 69. [Bobby] Crues and Hauser. In fact I played wih Crues there in Amarillo. And when it got up to . . . 60 . . . What the hell was it? 60. I got up to 60, and one night I got four. The season was kind of playing out on me. And I really— up to the night I hit those four, that old record of 69 really wasn't in my mind. Because I didn't think I had enough time.

There'd been a few things in the paper about the possibility of this and that, but until the night I got four, and I forget where that put me in the count—on up to about 68, I think, something like that. And then it became a real possibility, because we had, I don't know, four or five games left. Something like that.

And then when I tied the damn thing, at 69, we went on the road, at Big Spring, and then we had a doubleheader that closed out the season, in Artesia.

At Big Spring I didn't get any. Then we went into Artesia, and the manager over there was Jimmie Adair. He'd been a big league coach and everything else. He came over before the game, and I kind of had a bad experience over there at Big Spring, and he had heard about it. They wouldn't pitch to me. I either hit a bad pitch or nothing. They just wouldn't pitch to me at all.

So Jimmie Adair came over and told me he knew Hauser and had played with him, or against him, or something, but he knew Hauser, and he said, "I'll tell you one thing. I heard what went on in Big Spring, the way they horsed you around. But," he said, "we're going to pitch to you. We're not going to walk you. We'll give you a chance anyway." He said, "Good luck." So that's the way it was left.

The league standings were all set. Artesia was the number-one club in the league that year. They were number one and we were— in fact, we were second, I think. We finished second, but we were far enough behind that a doubleheader didn't make any difference. We couldn't go up and they couldn't go down. So the manager put me in the leadoff position to get more times at bat. He did it at Big Spring too, but it didn't do any good.

Well, anyway, there in Artesia, I got one the first damn time up. Leading off the game. And then in the second game I got two more. And that was it. [Laughs.]

"Joe Hauser said he met the umpire who worked the plate that day, and the umpire told him that the pitchers were really working on you."

As far as I was concerned they were. They were trying to get me out legitimately. Because Jimmie Adair told them they'd better not walk me.

"OK, one question: What's it been like for you to have done that?"

Oh, it's a . . . I have a good feeling about it, of course. It's not earth-shaking, or anything like that. I guess it's more of a trivia damn thing than anything else.

"But you're proud of it."

Yeah. If somebody gets hot, hits a bunch of home runs, or something like that, I'll get calls. They'll want my opinion or something. That's when I hear about it more than other times. Or if an article comes out in a magazine or a newspaper.

"So overall it hasn't been a bother. You feel good about it."

Yes. It's self-satisfying, and I quit on a happy note. I'll put it that way. I was satisfied when I quit.

Joe Willis Bauman

Born April 17, 1922, Welch, OK.
Batted left, threw left. Height: 6' 5". Weight: 235 lbs.

Year	Club	League	Position	G	AB	R	H	2B	3B	HR	RBI	BB	SB	BA
1941	Newport	Northeast Arkansas	1B	59	195	29	42	5	1	3	26	35	1	.215
	Little Rock	Southern Association	1B	3	10	0	0	0	0	0	0	—	0	.000
1942							(not in organized baseball)							
1943–45							(military service)							
1946	Amarillo	West Texas-New Mexico	1B	136	499	137	150	22	4	48*	159	109	3	.301
1947	Amarillo	West Texas-New Mexico	1B	130	432	142	151	45	2	38	127	151	3	.350
1948	Milwaukee	American Association	1B	1	1	0	0	0	0	0	0	—	0	.000
	Hartford	Eastern	1B	98	276	38	76	13	3	10	53	55	0	.275
1949–51							(not in organized baseball)							
1952	Artesia	Longhorn	1B	139	469	144	176	21	0	50*	157*	148*	2	.375
1953	Artesia	Longhorn	1B	132	463	135*	172	43	1	53*	141	130*	4	.371
1954	Roswell	Longhorn	1B	138	498	188*	199	35	3	72*	224*	150*	4	.400*
1955	Roswell	Longhorn	1B	131	453	118	152	32	3	46*	132	132*	1	.336
1956	Roswell	Southwestern	1B	52	167	51	48	5	0	17	38	64	0	.287
		Minor League totals		1019	3463	982	1166	221	17	337	1057	974	18	.337

*Led league

10

ON THE MOUND AT 55

BRUNO HAAS

There's a book known to autograph collectors that lists the addresses of all past and present major league baseball players—even if they played in only one game. Roman "Lefty" Bertrand's major league career consisted of exactly one game, and because of that I was able to track him down and ask him some questions about his former manager, a forgotten but colorful old gent named Bruno Haas. When asked if others had called about Bruno Haas, he replied, "You're the first." Bertrand, who knew Haas in the 1930s, is now in his late 80s.

Besides Lefty Bertrand, I have many others to thank for their help with this chapter, including former players Gene Corbett and Les Munns and several reference librarians, most notably Greg Gilstrap of the Fargo, North Dakota, public library, who sent me information on an absurd minor league all-star game the likes of which will probably never be seen again.

Bruno Haas was a player who could easily be overlooked but who, on close inspection, can be seen to have experienced a truly fascinating baseball career. He knew the ups and downs of baseball and was a member of one of the worst teams in major league history. We'll start his story there.

I love looking at the stats for the 1915 Philadelphia Athletics. Cecil "Squiz" Pillion, 21 years old, pitched in two games, gave up 10 hits in 5.1 innings, and never played in the majors again. Walter "Gee, Liver" Ancker, 21 years old, pitched in four games and gave up 17 walks and 19 hits in 17.2 innings, and never pitched again. Bob "Ike"

Cone, 21 years old, started one game and was taken out after giving up five hits and three runs in two-thirds of an inning (leaving Cone with a lifetime ERA of 40.50). Tom "Tink" Turner was a starting pitcher who gave up five hits and three walks in two innings, and that was it. He never pitched again.

But the star of the show was a native of Worcester, Massachusetts, named Bruno Philip Haas. Bruno Haas appeared in six games, giving up 23 hits and 28 walks in 14.1 innings. Haas, who never played in a major league game after 1915, also played a few games in the outfield, and he performed just as poorly at the plate as he did on the mound; he had one hit in 18 at bats for a lifetime batting average of .056.

Connie Mack used 27 pitchers in 1915—a major league record. (The 1962 Mets, another truly awful team, only used 17.) Even more remarkable—or weird—is that 12 of the team's pitchers made their only major league appearances in 1915. Ten of them were unable to register a single victory. None of the 12 threw a shutout. One of Mack's rookie pitchers in 1915, 27-year-old Jack Nabors, went 0–5. Nabors, however, was invited back for the 1916 season and was able to win one ball game. However, he lost 20 games and ended with a career record of 1–25.

The 1915 Mackmen had a team ERA of 4.33, which may not sound so bad, but remember that it happened during the dead ball period. The second worst ERA in the American League was 3.13. But it wasn't only on the mound that the team stank. The Athletics were second worst in the league at the plate, hitting .237. The team with the lowest batting average was New York, at .233. At least the Yankees had a decent fielding team. They led the league in fielding average and committed only 217 errors. The team that led the league in errors was . . . you guessed it.

The most amazing bit of information is that the Philadelphia Athletics, 1915's last-place club (58 games out of first), had won the American League pennant the year before. No other team in major league history has ever fallen so far in one year. (They went from a record of 99–53 in 1914 to 43–109 in 1915—a drop of 56 wins.)

So what the heck happened? (We'll get to Bruno Haas in a minute. This all ties together. Trust me.) What happened was that

Connie Mack sold or traded most of the star players from his 1914 pennant-winning team. We won't go into all the reasons—or theories—why Mack took such drastic action, but we will say that it doesn't seem to make a whole lot of sense. Some of the moves, okay, but not all of them.

Pitchers Chief Bender, Eddie Plank, and Jack Coombs, who together had accounted for 592 victories during their illustrious careers—all for the Athletics—were released in November of 1914, and a couple of weeks later Mack's number-one offensive weapon (and solid fielder) Eddie Collins was sold to the White Sox. Bender and Plank were just about at the end of the line but not completely through. It was believed they were about to sign with Federal League teams, which they in fact did shortly after being released. Coombs had been having health problems, but he joined Brooklyn and rebounded. Mack dumped Collins's high salary and brought in a reported $50,000. But Collins was only 27 at the time and had many great years still ahead of him. Perhaps the dumbest move made by Mack was selling Herb Pennock. Pennock went to the Red Sox June 3, 1915, for the astonishingly low price of $1,500 and then went on to pitch 18 more seasons during his Hall of Fame career.

Frank Baker, another bona fide star, informed Mack that he wasn't interested in jumping to the Federal League, but he did want to receive what he felt was a fair salary. Mack explained that the team hadn't drawn exceedingly well in 1914—few teams in the country did during that period—and that no raise was forthcoming, leaving the famous 29-year-old slugger as a holdout for the entire 1915 season. Mack announced in early June of 1915 that the Baker situation was "a dead issue." He then said he had lined up a couple of hot prospects to replace Baker at third base, including Fred "King" Lear. In Lear's first game, the collegian was inserted as a late-inning defensive replacement, and when Burt Shotton sprinted toward third on a steal attempt, Lear got the throw in time but was hung out to dry as the veteran Shotton slid safely around him. The heralded Lear was gone a few days later.

And that's how things were for the Philadelphia Athletics in 1915. They couldn't field, they couldn't hit, they couldn't pitch. Keep in mind that a fine young pitcher who Mack had been offered in 1914, Babe Ruth, was on his way to an 18–8 season over in Boston while Mack was scouring the country for a handful of prospects who could do reasonable impersonations of major league pitchers. And Ernie Shore, the man Jack Dunn of Baltimore had tried to package with Ruth for $20,000 or possibly less, was going one better than his teammate Ruth at 19–8.

Meanwhile, in Worcester, Massachusetts, Connie Mack's son Roy was attending a prep school, the Worcester Academy. Young Roy was the manager of the school baseball team, and he wrote his dad about the star of the team, a stocky left-hander with a huge barrel chest and long arms who threw hard, a fellow named Bruno Haas.

And so it came to be that, on June 23, 1915, in the midst of that terrible season, prep schooler Bruno Haas took the mound for the woeful Philadelphia Athletics in the second game of a doubleheader. In the first game, another young pitcher had made his professional debut with the A's. Minot "Cap" Crowell, fresh from Brown University, took the mound in the opener and pitched a masterful game, giving up just three hits—all singles—but he lost in 10 innings when another one of Mack's subpar replacements for Home Run Baker at third threw the ball over the first baseman's head with two away and the bases loaded.

And now it was Haas's turn. Haas pitched a terrible game. He gave up 11 hits, committed an error, threw three wild pitches, and set an all-time major league record for walks—16—a record that still stands.

Sixteen walks in one game. What an awful game it was. *The Philadelphia Inquirer* reporter wrote, "We don't know whether 16 passes constitutes a big league record or not, but it is enough. We feel absolutely convinced of that."

The New York Times, after a glowing and lengthy appraisal of Cap Crowell's performance in the first game, added, "The second game—forget it."

However painful it must have been to watch Haas's debut—the final score was 15–7—there was one person in attendance who may actually have rooted for Haas to break the record. Carroll "Boardwalk" Brown, a Yankee pitcher sitting in the New York bull pen that day, was well aware that the previous record for walks in a game was

15—he was the pitcher who, two years earlier, had set the dubious mark.

But let's forget about that game and jump forward to 1946. The place: a small town in the Midwest—St. Cloud, Minnesota. The setting: a ballpark. It's the Northern League all-star game. The first-place St. Cloud Rox are playing a team made up of the top players from the other seven teams in the league. And out there on the mound is a stocky fellow with long arms, a 55-year-old left-hander named Bruno Philip Haas.

Haas, who started his professional career with that terrible game 31 years earlier is in trouble again. This time, it's the ninth inning, the bases are loaded, and no one is out. We're going to come back to this game later to see if Bruno Haas, with all his baseball experience and knowledge, can figure out how to get out of this very unpleasant predicament.

◆ ◆ ◆

The Bruno Haas story probably sounds like a clown show so far, but that's not an accurate portrayal. Haas was a character, as those who remember him will attest, but he was a likable character, and even though he pitched one of the worst games in major league history, his story is one of triumph.

After 1915 teams weren't exactly trying to outbid each other for Haas's services, and Connie Mack shipped the muscle-bound youngster to the low minors. He played for Wilkes-Barre in 1916 as an everyday outfielder and showed enough promise that the Chicago White Sox drafted him in the fall. The White Sox assigned Haas to Newark, in the International League in 1917, which was a big jump from Wilkes-Barre, and Haas had a fairly decent season.

Following a year in the military, where he trained as a Navy fighter pilot in a special program at MIT, Haas was purchased by the Milwaukee Brewers in the American Association. Before the 1920 season, Milwaukee traded Haas to the St. Paul Saints, also in the American Association, and that's where Haas became a fixture. For 11 years he played left field. For 11 years the fans loved him.

Haas was a good, solid hitter. He didn't strike out much and, according to testimonials written years ago, he had a knack for coming through in the clutch. He was originally a right-handed hitter exclusively, but around 1924 he started switch-hitting, and they say Bruno Haas was equally productive batting from either side of the plate. He averaged .322 for the 11 years he played in St. Paul, with a good amount of extra-base hits—mostly doubles and triples—while stealing about 20 bases a season.

Lefty Bertrand, who saw Haas play as a kid, remarked that he had a powerful arm. "And he could play that ball off the fence. He threw out more guys at second base than anybody else ever did." But the thing the fans liked best about Haas was his daredevil attitude. He wouldn't quit. A ball would be hit back toward the fence in left field, and Haas would crash into the wall while making the catch. And then he'd get up smiling. And he did it all the time.

There were also the "belly catches." Haas used a long narrow glove, a glove players back then called a "motorman's glove," and he was known for sliding on his belly, getting a mouthful of turf, and making the grab.

How popular was Bruno Haas? This is from *The St. Paul Pioneer Press* from 1929: "Pisa has its leaning tower, Egypt has its pyramids, and St. Paul has its Bruno!"

The team Haas played for, the St. Paul Saints, was a powerhouse in the American Association during the early 1920s. In 1920, Haas's first year with the Saints, the team set a record with 115 wins and a .701 winning percentage and played the fabled Baltimore Orioles of the International League—with Lefty Grove et al.—in the first-ever Little World Series. Pennant winners in 1922 and 1924 as well, the Saints beat the Orioles in the 1922 confrontation.

Haas's most memorable game for St. Paul may have been the game in 1926 in which he went six for six. Or maybe it was the day a prankster in Toledo shone a mirror in Bruno's eyes from the bleachers while Haas was at the plate. The date was June 12, 1928, and after he had an usher get the fan to knock it off, he belted a home run.

Joe Hauser remembered Bruno Haas: "He was a card. I played against him when he was at St. Paul. A good Triple A ballplayer. He hit that ball. He didn't strike out much. He had a good, solid body,

1915 Worcester Academy team captains; Bruno Haas is at far right. (*Courtesy of Worcester Public Library, reproduced photograph by Professional Photography by Tasse, Worcester, MA*)

like a wrestler. Strong. Had a head sitting right on his shoulders. No neck. He was a nice guy to talk to."

In the late 1920s Haas was slowing down a bit. He was still hitting pretty well, but he wasn't able to cover as much ground in the outfield as before. After a couple of years of his diminished play, St. Paul did the unthinkable and traded him to Toledo for a younger outfielder named Leroy "Cowboy" Jones.

Ernest Mehl wrote in *The Kansas City Star* at the time, "A visitor going to St. Paul next summer will hardly know the place, because it has lost one of its oldest landmarks." Writer Mehl went on to say, "He is perhaps the best-known player in the American Association. The reason is his daredevil feats are well known to the fans." Mehl, who obviously liked Haas and from all indications was a good friend of the ballplayer as the following little ribbing would suggest, added, "If Bruno had not gone into the baseball business he would have been one of those men who leap into tanks of water or he would have been a motor car racer or a parachute jumper. Or a bigamist." Mehl also wrote, "His face is dark, his eyes black and he presents an appearance to indicate he might be a bad customer when aroused. But to cap it all off, he lisps. This is most surprising in such a fellow."

Haas played the outfield for a few more years in various leagues and then, in late 1932, he announced that he was undertaking a new venture. At that time of great financial instability, many teams and even a few leagues were going out of business. But Haas, who was a free thinker as well as a free spirit, joined with a few partners to create a new minor league—the Northern League. It was a move that was widely talked about in baseball circles and was thought by most to be a truly insane undertaking. Said longtime sportswriter Vince Leah in 1973 in a fond reminiscence, "The scoffers thought Haas was stark raving mad to bring Organized Baseball (back to that part of the country and Canada) in the dark of the Depression."

Bruno Haas was an indomitable sort, and he knew what he was doing. The Northern League flourished.

The Winnipeg franchise was Haas's, and it was the most profitable team in the league. Haas, besides being the owner, managed the club and also played the outfield on occasion. He even pitched a few games. A check of the records indicates that his inability to throw strikes was a characteristic he discarded when he left Philadelphia.

Gene Corbett grew up in St. Paul and as a kid used to hang around the ballpark, where he met Bruno Haas and other members of the St. Paul team. Corbett was a promising sandlotter, and St. Paul signed him to a contract after high school. However, a short while later, the team sent him a letter stating they couldn't take him after all because money was just too tight. But they told Corbett about Bruno Haas and the new league and suggested he attend a try-out camp Haas was planning to hold at a St. Paul ball field the next spring. Said Corbett, "There were over 400 guys trying out for that one team. There were 15 or 16 first basemen. And that was my position." Corbett made the team and went on to become one of the stars of the Northern League for the Winnipeg Maroons, leading in hits and home runs in 1933 and RBIS in 1935.

Corbett said, "We were called 'The Yankees of the Northern League,' because we had a bus, an old Greyhound bus. Some of the

other teams would travel in school buses, or even station wagons—
not even station wagons. They had a name for them—gutwrenchers—
or something like that. Straight-back seats. Can you imagine taking a
500 mile bus ride on that? Our bus had soft seats and plenty of
room."

Bruno Haas was well liked by his players but considered something of an eccentric. "He was different," said Lefty Bertrand. Once
in a while after driving for eight or nine hours, the Winnipeg team
would spend a night in St. Paul, where Haas, after piloting the bus
all day would unwind for a few hours, if you can imagine this, by
hopping into his car and taking a drive.

"That's Bruno," said Bertrand.

When the Northern League started in 1933, professional baseball hadn't been played in Winnipeg for several years, and the concept of a doubleheader seemed foreign to the fans. Haas was pinch-
ing pennies left and right, and he worked out a new system for
doubleheaders. After the first game, Haas had the ushers march the
customers out of the stadium (Sherburn Park). Then the fans, who
apparently didn't mind the inconvenience, would get back in line to
pay again to see the second game.

Home plate in Sherburn Park was located close to the stands,
and many a foul ball cleared the roof and left the park. Haas had a
reputation for scurrying out onto Portage Avenue during batting
practice and chasing the costly baseballs. Vince Leah wrote that, on
one occasion, Haas was underneath the stands shaving when he
heard a ball leave the park. He ran out after it, lathered up and shirt-
less, still carrying a razor. According to Leah, writing in the *Winnipeg
Free Press* in 1969, "A frightened passerby called the police, so the
story goes, thinking a wild man was loose."

Despite Bruno's peculiarities, or perhaps because of them, he
became as popular in Winnipeg as he had been in St. Paul. And his
players were treated royally. Gene Corbett remembered how the
young players would spend off evenings hanging out at D. J. Berry-
hill's Drugstore where they made friends with the locals. Between
games of a doubleheader, the players would walk the two blocks to
the drugstore—in uniform—to have a quick snack. "Those were

the days," said Corbett. "We were treated like kings." Bruno's players were even admitted free to the movie theaters in Winnipeg. All they had to do, said Corbett, was walk up to the cashier and announce, "I'm a Winnipeg Maroon!"

During games Haas was known for getting into hot water with the umpires—a characteristic that seems to crop up with many minor league managers. Eugene Fitzgerald, a writer for the *Fargo* (North Dakota) *Forum*, who in 1952 called Bruno Haas "unquestionably the most colorful character to play in the Northern League since its revival in 1933," wrote about Haas and his relationship with the umps:

> Bruno had a cute way of baiting umpires. One incident which took place in [Fargo's] Barnett Field when he was manager at Winnipeg will never be forgotten.
>
> Amby Moran, most colorful of the arbiters to work in the Northern League, had told Bruno not to charge the plate and protest again. "If I hear one more peep out of you I'll run you," he warned Bruno.
>
> Moran ordered Bruno to the bench. As he walked back to the accompaniment of booing, he stopped suddenly. When there was quiet he said in a high-pitched voice which could be heard through the stands: "Peep." Nothing more. Moran ordered him from the park and Bruno went satisfied. He had given the crowd a good show.

Roman "Lefty" Bertrand, picked up from a rival Northern League team during the middle of the 1934 season, and a 19-game winner for Haas in 1935, recalled how Haas was once thumbed for calling the umpire "a rooster-fish." Bertrand said that in the clubhouse after the game, the players—who were all puzzled by the unusual term—gathered around Haas to hear the explanation. Haas, Bertrand said, told them that a fish is sometimes called a sucker, and a rooster is called a . . .

Haas didn't get thrown out of every game but enough of them, and it may have cost the team the pennant in 1934. The Maroons were in the race down to the wire, but Haas, as excitable as ever, couldn't contain himself and got tossed during almost every game the last week of the season.

That's why Bruno Haas fired Bruno Haas. He brought in an old friend from American Association days, Wes Griffen, who was also considered a hothead but one who knew where to draw the line, and Haas concerned himself more with front office duties. Lefty Bertrand said this move by Haas was well thought out, and because of it the 1935 team was able to play up to its level of ability—and they indeed did win the league championship, with Gene Corbett and Bertrand contributing heavily. After the season the two players were sold together to the Philadelphia Phillies, where they were able to get a glimpse of life in the big leagues.

Bertrand, who along with Gene Corbett remembers Bruno Haas as a great guy to play for "because of his humor," also mentioned that Haas, interestingly, didn't seem to care at all about his lisp. He wasn't self-conscious about it and he didn't speak softly. His voice boomed. It was all part of his personality, all part of the package.

Haas didn't smoke or drink. But he was a little on the blue side with his language. "He told a lot of stories," said Bertrand. "But they were all a little off-color." And when he was upset, the players would invariably hear him mutter, "Dee-thuth Cryth!"

And now it's time to return to the story we mentioned briefly earlier. In 1946 Haas, after selling his interest in the Winnipeg team following the 1938 season and being in and out of baseball during the next few years, was managing another Northern League team, the Fargo-Moorhead Twins. During the middle of the season, the all-star game was to be played in St. Cloud, Minnesota, and Bruno Haas was named the manager.

Through the first eight innings, Haas used four pitchers, allowing each to throw two innings a piece. The players were mostly young—in their late teens and early twenties—and Bruno Haas, ever the showman, decided to give the players and fans something to smile about. In the ninth inning, he walked to the mound and began warming up to pitch.

Earlier in his career he had taken as many as five years off his age, but now he admitted the truth: he was 55 years old. He had played a little since 1933, but not much. He had pitched a little, done some pinch hitting, and filled in a few times in the outfield. Records are somewhat sketchy, but he played 20 games in 1942 (and may or may not have pitched in a few games that year), and then he pitched in a couple of games in 1946—and was hit hard.

Lefty Bertrand remembers Haas put on an exhibition in 1934, between halves of a split season, pitching a 1–0 victory over a rival manager. "He threw pretty hard," said Bertrand. "He had a good fastball and a forkball." But that was 12 years earlier. This time, at 55, Haas had gone too far. But, as they say, "That's Bruno." There was no stopping the guy.

So Haas walked to the mound. He also made two other changes. He brought in Lynn King, one of his coaches, and had him replace the youngster at first base. He had the other coach, Rae Blaemire, go behind the plate to do the catching.

Haas had nothing that day except a lot of nerve, and even that was leaving him fast as he gave up two quick singles to open the ninth. As he was running out of steam, maybe it was for old-time's sake, he walked a batter. And then he paused.

He looked at third and saw a young man in his prime leading off the base, poised to sprint home. He saw the same situation at second and first. What could have been going on in his mind as he surveyed the disaster he had created? Perhaps he was remembering the slogan of his old school in New England, the Worcester Academy: "Achieve the Honorable." More likely, he was thinking something along the lines of, "You old fool! What the hell are you doing out here? Dee-thuth Cryth!"

When Bruno finally let the pitch go, he saw the batter make a mighty swing and top the ball toward third. Haas did a reasonable facsimile of someone sprinting and pounced on that little dribbler. Pitchers often slip trying to make this play, but he flipped the ball to the catcher, Blaemire, who tagged the plate for the force and fired the ball to first, completing an electrifying (for Bruno) double play!

And then Lynn King, the third old guy on the field and the guy holding the ball at first, saw in a flash that the runner who started at second base on the play was rounding third and flying toward the plate. Then came the throw—yes! Triple play! So Bruno Haas, who started his professional baseball career with an unforgettably awful performance, was able to end it on a wonderfully high note.

According to a newspaper account, Haas ran in, all smiles, and jumped on his catcher, and the two stood there and hugged each other as the players ran toward them and the fans went nuts.

Bruno Philip Haas

Born May 5, 1891, Shrewsbury, MA. Died June 5, 1952, Sarasota, FL.
Batted both, threw left. Height: 5'9". Weight: 185 lbs.

Year	Club	League	Position	G	AB	R	H	2B	3B	HR	RBI	SB	BA
1915	Philadelphia	American	P–OF	12	18	1	1	0	0	0	0	0	.056
1916	Wilkes–Barre	New York State	OF–3B	125	472	64	141	23	7	3		25	.299
1917	Newark	International	OF	132	497	52	127	20	8	5		18	.256
1918			(military service)										
1919	Milwaukee	American Association	OF	129	459	76	135	20	8	7	64	13	.294
1920	St. Paul	American Association	OF–2B–P	130	446	73	137	24	5	11	72	12	.307
1921	St. Paul	American Association	OF–2B	144	527	100	171	27	7	6	90	14	.324
1922	St. Paul	American Association	OF–1B	146	547	105	181	35	14	8	111	24	.331
1923	St. Paul	American Association	OF	156	554	112	186	37	15	14	100	22	.336
1924	St. Paul	American Association	OF	155	536	85	157	22	13	11	78	24	.293
1925	St. Paul	American Association	OF–P	117	419	70	133	24	6	10	76	18	.317
1926	St. Paul	American Association	OF	158	590	75	194	51	8	8	63	20	.329
1927	St. Paul	American Association	OF	115	440	64	147	32	5	6	76	24	.334
1928	St. Paul	American Association	OF–1B	151	564	76	185	34	5	10	60	18	.328
1929	St. Paul	American Association	OF	135	510	56	151	31	4	3	40	6	.296
1930	St. Paul	American Association	OF	82	262	40	98	11	5	3	73	6	.374
1931	Toledo/Milwaukee	American Association	OF	138	488	65	139	26	2	6	58	6	.285
1932	New Orleans	Southern Association	OF	84	320	49	98	13	5	6	17	3	.306
	Des Moines	Western	OF	26	82	8	18	7	1	0		2	.220
1933	Winnipeg	Northern	OF–P	49	141	14	34	6	1	4	19	3	.241

Year	Team	League											
1934–36	Winnipeg	Northern	(manager—did not play)										
1937	Winnipeg	Northern	P–OF	29	41	9	10	3	1	2	9	0	.196
1938	Winnipeg	Northern	P–OF	24	48	4	14	3	0	1	6	0	.292
1939–41			(not in organized baseball)										
1942	Grand Forks	Northern	P–OF	20	25	1	4	1	0	0	3	0	.160
1943–45			(not in organized baseball)										
1946	Fargo-Moorhead	Northern	P	3	2	0	1	1	0	0	0	0	.500
	Major League totals			12	18	1	1	0	0	0	0	0	.056
	Minor League totals			2246	7980	1198	2461	451	120	124	1015	252	.308

Pitching Record

Year	Team	League	G	IP	W	L	PCT.	H	SO	BB	ERA
1915	Philadelphia	American	6	14.1	0	1	.000	23	7	28	11.93
1920	St. Paul	American Association	1		1	0	1.000				
1925	St. Paul	American Association	1		0	1	.000				
1933	Winnipeg	Northern	13	61	3	0	1.000	70	49	15	
1937	Winnipeg	Northern	13	56	1	4	.200	54	28	18	3.05
1938	Winnipeg	Northern	13	53	2	3	.400	49	27	21	
1942	Grand Forks	Northern	?								
1946	Fargo-Moorhead	Northern	3	9	1	0	1.000	13	5	2	

II

He Didn't Look Like Much of a Hitter (Looks Can Be Deceiving)

OSCAR ECKHARDT

Here's something a little different. A good-natured and eccentric grandfather tells his grandson a true story about a fellow Texan. The grandson replies, "Goo."

Now, Jimmie, I know you're not even a year old, and I know you don't understand a word your old grandpa is yakking about, but while your momma is out doing her errands, I think I'll just tell you about my favorite baseball player, a fellow by the name of Oscar Eckhardt. What's that? "Goo?" Oh you like baseball! Yes, yes, good. Maybe I'll give you my scrapbook in a couple of years. I don't know how long I'm gonna be around, you know. Oh, you don't want to hear about that. Fair enough.

Now, Oscar Eckhardt was from around here. Yes, a fellow Texan. From over in Yorktown. And what upsets me is that hardly anybody remembers him anymore. That's why I'm telling you about him, Jimmie. See, we've got to keep the memory of Oscar Eckhardt alive! Yes. What's that? Well, crawl over and get it. There you go.

We called him Ossie, or Os, and when he got in the pros they called him "Ox." Oscar the Ox. Where he got started was in Austin at the University of Texas. Big man on campus. Oscar was quite an athlete. He did everything, you know. Baseball. Football. Basketball. He did a little pitching. Would have had a no-hitter one day. What? Jimmie, I'll pull that scrapbook out right now and prove it! Oh, you believe me. That's my boy. Oscar would have had a no-hitter. Well, maybe. He pitched six innings and didn't give up a hit and didn't walk nobody. Nobody, Jimmie! Yet the coach took him out.

But football was the rage, as it is these days, and Mr. Oscar Eckhardt was no slouch. He was voted Most Valuable Player in the Southwestern Conference, if that gives you an idea. He played halfback, and they couldn't stop him. Big and fast. He played a little pro football, later, you know. And he could kick! Best punter I ever seen. I wouldn't say the ball disappeared when he gave it the boot, but it did get awful small up there, awful small. The guys would—hey! Get that out of your mouth! Yes, thank you.

So ol' Oscar played pros. Did he ever. I'm talking baseball, now, sonny. The Tigers wanted him, and he signed with 'em, but there was some kind of a problem with the contract, and Oscar ended up having to sit out two years. He played a couple of games in Austin, as I recollect it, then sat out those two years, yes, and then he played a full season in the Western League, with Wichita and Amarillo. How did he do? Hit about .370, .380. Good enough for you? And he went on to Seattle, which, as you know, was in the Pacific Coast League. And he hit about .350. So, the word was out: Oscar the Ox was a hitter.

Detroit owned his contract, and they sent Oscar to Beaumont in 1930 and—hold on to your hat!—he led the league. I told you he was a hitter. How was he as a base runner? He was stealing maybe 15, 20 bases a year. Didn't have a lot of power. Hit a lot of doubles—50, 55 in his best years. You're right. That is a lot.

Now, Jimmie, you've probably never heard of the San Francisco Missions. No? Well, they were in the Pacific Coast League, the same time as the Seals. Yeah, I knew you'd heard of the Seals, and the Missions bought Ossie's contract in 1931. The Pacific Coast League, or "p-c-l," was a very high level of ball. No slouches. Well, not many.

Oscar "Ox" Eckhardt. This awkward-looking hitter once batted .414 in the Pacific Coast League. Two years later, in 1935, Eckhardt edged out Joe DiMaggio for the league batting title, .399 to .398. (© *Brace Photo*)

And our hero, Mr. Ox, led that high class league in hitting in 1931 and, wait, there's more, he led in 1932 and 1933, and in 1934 he just missed it. Oh, his average was way down that year, at .378. Maybe Oscar got sorry for the other fella and let him win it. Don't look at me that way. Okay, the other guy won it fair and square.

But do you see what I'm trying to tell you? This guy Oscar Eckhardt was one heck of a hitter. And he never became a regular in the majors. Well, there's a couple of reasons, and none of them make any sense to me. Not really. Oscar belonged up there. That's for sure. That's for—don't tell your momma I said this—that's for *damn* sure.

Eckhardt had a couple of shots with Detroit in spring training and with the Boston Braves. Oh! What a chance they gave him! Eight at bats! Eight lousy at bats. Did he strike out every time or something? No. He had a couple of hits.

Eckhardt was just a fair fielder, not bad but not great. His arm was good. It probably hurt him that he didn't hit for much power. But it was his batting style that drove managers crazy. He was a left-handed hitter, and he kind of fell away from the plate when he hit, which didn't look too good. And he bent his legs; it almost looked like he was trying to sit down. So that looked bad.

And they didn't like it that he hit everything to left field. He just couldn't pull the ball. Well, who cares? Right. He got on base all the time. The guy should have played in the majors for a long time.

You know, he might have stuck with the Braves, that was in 1932, but the Missions wanted him back. They were in last place, losing a lot of games, and they made a deal to bring Eckhardt back. What did Eckhardt think about going back to the Missions? Not much, and he told 'em so.

Oh, you're right! I didn't tell you about 1935! Before I forget, in 1933, Ox Eckhardt set the all-time PCL record for batting—are you ready for this?—with an average of .414.

But you asked about 1935. Yes, of course he led the PCL in hitting that year. I know your math isn't too good yet. Why yes, little Jim, that's four years out of five! Ox Eckhardt led the league in batting four years out of five. So why isn't he famous? That I don't understand, Jimmie. Like I said, people in his hometown don't even know who he was.

Oh, yeah, he's dead. Been dead since 1951. He was only 49. How'd it happen? Heart attack. He was on his horse. Died with his boots on. Yeah, over in Yorktown. Same place as he was born. Yeah, I knew him. A little bit. He was older than me though. But let me tell you about 1935. Eckhardt was battling Joe DiMaggio for the batting championship, and it got down to the last day of the season, a doubleheader. Eckhardt and the Missions were playing two in Hollywood against the Stars. DiMaggio and the Seals had a twin bill in Seattle.

Now, I don't get this, because Ox Eckhardt was a popular player, but the Seattle boys tried to help Mr. DiMaggio win the championship. No, no, the Black Sox was something else, and this wasn't really that big a deal. You know, my theory is that the Seattle players were just bored, and this gave them something to do. Yes, I really believe that. What they did was, every time DiMaggio hit the ball, they'd turn around and run the other way. You're giving me that look again. Do you want the truth, or do you want a fascinating story? The truth, OK. They just didn't try very hard. And DiMaggio didn't like it one bit. He even went to the official scorer and asked him to change a couple of hits to errors. He didn't want to win the batting championship that bad. Not that way.

But Eckhardt went four for five in the first game of his doubleheader, and that was all he needed, and his manager sat him out for the nightcap. Rack up another batting championship for our fellow Texan.

You want to do something else for a while? You want me to bring out that scrapbook? No, you can't drool on it! These are sacred memories. My lord, child, ain't you had no proper upbringing? Don't cry. I'm just—hold on a second. Thank God for that bottle. So what do you want to do when you grow up? You don't know? There's no hurry, son. Enjoy your childhood. And your babyhood. And eat a lot of candy. That's the best advice I can give you. I know you're too young to understand how wonderful candy is, but when you grow up a little, maybe in a few months or a year, I'm not really sure, you're gonna find the wonders of candy. No, no, don't tell your momma I told you about that.

Jimmie's grandpa forgot to mention that Ox Eckhardt also had a brief trial with Brooklyn early in 1936 when he was 34. Eckhardt, a notorious late starter,

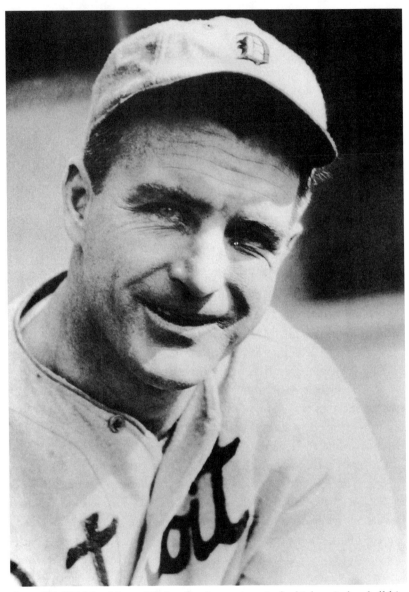

Oscar "Ox" Eckhardt's .365 lifetime batting average is the highest in baseball history. (*Courtesy of National Baseball Hall of Fame Library & Archive, Cooperstown, NY*)

*batted .182 in 16 games. He retired in 1940 after a stint with Dallas, having
compiled a career batting average of .365, the highest in the history of pro ball.*

From the Austin American, 1936:

In the annual discussion of the Oscar Eckhardt case, i.e., why
Oscar the Ox did not draw a term or at least a fair trial in the
major leagues, no better reason for the moguls' mistakes was
ever advanced than that the big Austin slugger looks so down-
right awkward and unorthodox at the plate nobody believed
he could possibly hit a lick.

Now that Oscar is assailing the fences in Clearwater,
Florida, for Casey Stengel's daffy Dodgers, and it appears the
ex-U.T. football hero will get his first big chance at 34, the
above theory is substantiated by a story in the *New York Post,*
written by Jerry Mitchell soon after Eckhardt struck camp:

Head Bowed

CLEARWATER, Fla.—Oscar the Ox was hitting, but
Casey Stengel sat in the dugout with his eyes tightly closed.
It seemed as though he didn't care what the Ox, otherwise
Oscar G. Eckhardt, the 34-year-old recruit who led the
Pacific Coast league in hitting last season, did up there.

The Professor wasn't sleeping on the job because,
although he seemed to nap while the Ox was making pre-
liminary passes at the pitcher with a big black stick, he
opened his eyes at the crack of the bat and grinned as the
ball bulleted into left field or through the box. He seemed
to be playing some sort of game with himself down there
in the dugout.

The Professor was merely following instructions, however. "Gabby Street and other guys on the coast told me that
this is the only way to watch this guy hit," he explained.
"You gotta close your eyes and bow your head when he
swings, then look up when you hear the wallop and ask
somebody where the ball went. Otherwise you're liable to
run up there and grab his bat and say, 'Fer gosh-shakes, that

ain't the way to hit. Here, watch me.'—and start showing him how an ordinary human bein' swings at a ball.

"They were right, too. Just look at him hittin'. The only one I ever remember hittin' anything like that was Ike Boone. He's almost on top of the plate, and when he swings he falls away from it. See how he holds his bat? He cuts at a ball—buggywhips it. Watch him awhile and you'll see him sorta squat as he swings. Sometimes he's on his knees when he hits. Seems to do everything wrong—but he can hit, there's no mistakin' that. Seems to hit to left and left center and through the left side of the infield.

"They said he was something of a push hitter, but I don't think so," continued the Professor. "He's got some power—more than Boone, for example. Watch this Osborne pitch to him; he was on the same club. He's mighty careful out there, doesn't wanna get one knocked down his throat. Confidentially, that's why I don't like to buy those Coast league pitchers—most of 'em got bad knees from bein' hit by this Eckhardt's shots through the box. Yeah, honest." Anyway, Oscar the Ox, who has shown all of his widely advertised hitting ability, good speed going down the line to first base and less awkwardness in the outfield than had been expected, was leading off in the batting order and playing left field for the regulars in the first camp scrimmage with the yannigans. If he continues to show more of the same he will be the Dodgers' left fielder and first batsman on April 14 at the polo grounds."

Oscar the Ox hopes so, but he seems a little afraid that he won't be in the proper working order in time. "I never hit in the spring," he says. "My timing, everything, seems off, no matter how I try, and I get worse when I start pressing. I guess that's what cost me a major league job the other two times I was up with Detroit and the Braves. I looked so bad in the spring. I sure hope I can get started early this time; I'm no youngster and probably won't get a major league chance again."

Doggone!

It was probably the complications that developed when he came to camp accompanied by his wife and 10-year-old Belgian police dog that put the big, serious Texan in a bit of a blue mood, however. He couldn't take the dog into the hotel, and not having children, couldn't obtain the club's permission to live outside, either.

"It may sound like a joke to you fellas," he said, "but when you got a dog like that with you on the ranch all these years you get mighty attached to it. Why, back in my place at Yorktown—that's near San Antonio—I put a small mattress next to my bed and Ring sleeps on it. I have her outside now, but it seems worse than shootin' her. We've never been separated."

The Professor hopes that no one else shows up with livestock. Life among the Dodgers would be still more complicated if Van Mungo checked in with some of his cattle and bird dogs, or Joe Stripp arrived in a sulky behind his trotter, Casey Stengel IV.

From the San Francisco Call-Bulletin, *September 10, 1935:*

Eckhardt was almost the goat and then was the hero of a quaint play in the finale of the Red Angel series yesterday. In the second game, which the Reds won, 6 to 5, Eckhardt was on third base and Berger on second when Beck walked. Oscar started to saunter home, under the impression, presumably, that the bags were filled and he was being forced in.

The Angels in their surprise at discovering a stray on the path, let him escape safely back to third. Then, while they were still dumbfounded by the extraordinary procedure, Eckhardt dashed off the bag again and stole home.

Oscar George (Ox) Eckhardt

Born December 23, 1901, Yorktown, TX. Died April 22, 1951, Yorktown, TX.
Batted left, threw right. Height: 6' 1". Weight: 190 lbs.

Year	Club	League	Position	G	AB	R	H	2B	3B	HR	RBI	SB	BA
1925	Austin	Texas Association	OF	2	7	1	2	0	0	0	0	0	.286
1926–27							(not in organized baseball)						
1928	Wichita/Amarillo	Western	OF	127	490	91	184	32	27*	3	—	20	.376
1929	Seattle	Pacific Coast	OF	161	571	84	202	35	17*	7	70	16	.354
1930	Beaumont	Texas	OF	147	573	99	217*	55*	5	8	83	19	.379*
1931	Missions (SF)	Pacific Coast	OF	185	745	129	275*	52	10	7	117	9	.369*
1932	Boston	National	PH	8	8	1	2	0	0	0	1	0	.250
	Missions (SF)	Pacific Coast	OF	134	539	80	200	33	13	5	82	15	.371*
1933	Missions (SF)	Pacific Coast	OF	189*	760	145	315*	56	16	12	143	15	.414*
1934	Missions (SF)	Pacific Coast	OF	184	707	126	267	36	11	6	106	7	.378
1935	Missions (SF)	Pacific Coast	OF-P	172	710	149	283*	40	11	2	114	8	.399*
1936	Brooklyn	National	OF	16	44	5	8	1	0	1	6	0	.182
	Indianapolis	American Association	OF	128	541	95	191	26	11	4	69	3	.353
1937	Indianapolis	American Association	OF	142	589	97	201	20	8	7	79	14	.341
1938	Toledo	American Association	OF	55	201	29	46	9	3	2	29	3	.229
	Beaumont	Texas	OF	72	279	43	108	19	7	0	43	4	.387
1939	Memphis	Southern Association	OF	124	482	61	174	26	4	2	80	6	.361
1940	Dallas	Texas	OF	104	369	46	108	16	3	1	22	1	.293
	Major League totals			24	52	6	10	1	0	1	7	0	.192
	Minor League totals			1926	7563	1275	2773	455	146	66	1037	140	.367

*Led league

12

REMEMBERING TED,
BABE HERMAN, AND
A BUNCH OF OTHER GUYS

WALLY HEBERT

Wally Hebert burst upon the majors in spectacular fashion, winning his first big league start and making headlines in sports pages across the country. The year was 1931, and Hebert hurled the lowly St. Louis Browns to victory over the powerful Philadelphia Athletics, who would go on to win their third straight American League pennant that year. It was the year Lefty Grove set the sports world abuzz by winning 16 consecutive ball games. Wally Hebert had plenty to say about that, as well as about facing Babe Ruth, Lou Gehrig, Al Simmons, and other sluggers. Hebert (pronounced A-bear), a native of Lake Charles, Louisiana, was interviewed for this book in 1995 at the age of 88. In 1998, at age 91, he told me by phone that he was still an active outdoorsman, sloshing around in hip boots in the muddy waters near his home fishing and hunting whenever possible.

WALLY HEBERT: I saw Lefty Grove trying to win his 17th straight game, in Philadelphia. The reason I remember it, we went into Canada and played an exhibition game. We got on the train to go to Philadelphia, and everybody who drank had a suitcase full of liquor.

We were all in our sleeper that night, and I had two or three bottles in my bag. They belonged to Walter Stewart. I didn't drink.

A police officer came in and said, "I don't guess any of you guys got any liquor in your bag." It was against the law to come across the line with any of that stuff. And old Dick Coffman, one of our pitchers, raised up and gave him a big Bronx cheer. Man, that cop made everybody dump everything out of their bag and onto the floor. And he picked up every one of them bottles. He was going to let us through, but Coffman gave him that big blast. So Bill Killefer told Coffman—he knew he was drunk—he told him, "Then you've got to pitch tomorrow against Grove." We all knew Lefty Grove was going after his 17th straight win, which would have been a new record. But in that game Oscar Melillo hit a line drive and their left fielder ran up on it, it went over his head, and a man scored from first. And we beat Grove 1–0. Dick Coffman won that ball game for the Browns.

That year Philadelphia won the pennant. I was a rookie, but I beat them a couple of times. Lucky, I guess.

I began my career in 1930 playing with a Gulf State Utility team here in Lake Charles. There was a man by the name of Cahill. He was scouting for the St. Louis Browns, and he sent me to Springfield, Missouri, in a Class A league. I won 15 games in that league there, and I went to spring training the next year with the St. Louis Browns. I went over there actually more to pitch batting practice, because they only had one other left-handed pitcher on the club, Walter Stewart. But I pitched a few games against other teams there, and I did good, so they kept me. I would have been better off if I'd a gone to Wichita Falls. That was in the Texas League. I'd have gotten to work regular there. But I stayed with St. Louis.

Even though Wally Hebert made it onto the St. Louis roster, manager Bill Killefer was reluctant to pitch the youngster and didn't use him in a league game until the season was several weeks old. But during the month of June, Hebert won four ball games and became one of the most talked about rookies in baseball.

I relieved against the Yankees and did good. I was in the lead. Bill Killefer, he figured I was so young I would probably choke up, so he had Sam Gray relieve me to pitch the last inning, and they beat him. So I didn't win that game. I didn't have a record on that game.

The first game I won was against Philadelphia. I won it 8–2, against Walberg. And then I pitched three or four games against the Yankees that year. I won one, and Lefty Gomez beat me 1–0 one game. And then, after that, I hurt my arm. After that it was mostly relief.

I hurt my arm just bad enough that I didn't have good control. I always had good control, all the time I pitched, except the last two years with St. Louis. The Browns traded me to Hollywood for a shortstop—Alan Strange I think his name was. I didn't feel bad at all about going to Hollywood. I hadn't been pitching regular with the Browns. And I went over there on the Coast where it was warm. Los Angeles was a good climate. San Diego was perfect. I always did like pitching in warm weather. I had a little trouble that first year with Hollywood, but after that I kinda got going.

Hebert pitched for the Hollywood Stars in 1934 and '35, and transferred with the team in 1936 to San Diego, playing on the original San Diego Padres. He won 147 games in nine years with that minor league franchise, including three 20-game seasons.

The last year I was there I had 33 complete ball games, and over 300 innings, and I won, I think it was 25 games. That includes two in the playoffs.

I went to the Pirates the next year, 1943, and my ERA there was 2.98. But it was a tough year. Frankie Frisch was our manager at Pittsburgh, and he believed a left-handed pitcher should only pitch against left-handed hitters. But I didn't have any trouble against the right-handers in the Coast League. I kept the curveball in on 'em. And they'd hit it on the ground. But under Frisch I didn't pitch regular, you know, like I had pitched on the Coast, and I didn't stay in good shape that way. So the next year I turned down my best contract, and I quit. My arm wasn't hurting or anything.

I had two kids to haul around, and during the 1943 year there were hardly any trains. That was a tough year for the wife to travel. At the end of the season my wife and kids had to travel back to Lake Charles with a bunch of people who had gone nuts in the service. They were on a train and gave 'em all kind of trouble. They had lost their minds, cracked up and all. And my wife had a hard time. The train people couldn't do anything with them. My wife said that finally a couple of Marine MPs got on there, and those guys shut up.

After a nine-year absence from the major leagues, Wally Hebert came back with the Pittsburgh Pirates in 1943. (© *Brace Photo*)

But we decided not to go back East the next year, because you couldn't get any trains anywhere hardly.

In 1944 the business manager of the Pirates came to Lake Charles to sign me up. I signed, but I told him I was going to wait, stay and get in shape over here, and report about two weeks before the season started. But things hadn't gotten any better, and my oldest daughter was about to start school that year, and I had a job here at Firestone, so I just stayed. Pittsburgh held my contract for about five years, but I never did go back.

◆ ◆ ◆

One of Wally Hebert's teammates back in the minors had been a young gangling kid, last name Williams, first name Ted.

Ted Williams broke in with us at San Diego. He and Bobby Doerr and George McDonald all broke in with us, right out of high school. I was there for their rookie year. When Ted Willams walked in, I thought he was a great big, old, loose, gawky-looking kid. And he could hit then. He played with me two years. He used to sit there and watch some of them guys hit, and he'd say, "Boy, I wish I could hit like that." But he was already a better hitter than they were.

The only thing is he didn't hustle too much after he failed to get a base hit. But Shellenback put him on the bench a couple of times, and he got over that. I was with the team the year Shellenback finally let him pitch, in Los Angeles. What happened was Ted Williams was pitching, and about three line drives hit the boards in center field. He came in and said, "I'm going to stick to the outfield."

◆ ◆ ◆

In a strange but true story that has been forgotten over time, comedian Joe E. Brown umpired the bases during a game played between Hollywood and the San Francisco Missions on the last day of the 1935 season. Songwriter Harry Ruby got into the act by replacing Bobby Doerr at second base in the fifth inning, and when Ruby came up with two out in the last inning, Joe E. Brown chased the pitcher off the mound and then had the outfielders and infielders sit around him near the mound while he warmed up to pitch using a comic windup he'd perfected over the years. The box score shows that Joe E. Brown struck out Harry Ruby and that the opposing pitcher was Wally Hebert.

I sure forgot about that. It was a league game? It must have been a game that didn't mean much. Harry Ruby? Oh, I remember him. He was a songwriter. I think he wrote "My Little Pumpchin" or something like that. He was a nice guy. But he wanted to play ball in the worst way, and he was the worst ballplayer that I ever saw. Joe E. Brown, he was pretty handy with a ball. He could handle a baseball good. Ruby played second base? I hope nobody hit one at him.

Our club made a movie out there, *Alibi Ike*, with Joe E. Brown. We divided up. We wore Yankee and Cub uniforms, but it was our regular spring training. And they were taking shots. And I guess I was supposed to have been Lefty Gomez, because I was a left-handed pitcher. And then Alibi Ike, he got captured in that movie by gangsters. And he came busting through that wall. That was the Hollywood ball club. We trained at Riverside, California. That's where they made that movie.

We must of worked about 15 days. Every day as we went out they'd give every ballplayer 10 dollars. And they gave the wives five dollars. The wives in the grandstand, clapping and all that, that was mostly the ballplayers' wives.

Joe E. Brown was the star pitcher in that movie. William Frawley was the manager of one of those clubs. And Olivia de Havilland, that girl, she was the star in it. They had another little redheaded girl in there too. I don't remember her name. It was a lot of fun.

When he busts through the wall, everybody runs. He had an old Model T car, and we all ran up to the car, and I put my foot on the running board. That's the only place I ever saw myself in that movie.

Jack Quinn, the old spitball pitcher, he was with us for a while in Hollywood. He relieved for us a couple of games, but he never did get going. So he didn't stay all year. The reason I remember him, the guys who were playing regular got to ride in the lower bunk on the train. He wasn't a regular, so Ced Durst put him in a top bunk. And he was sitting there moaning, and I said—I never did sleep on

the train—I said, "Hey, you can have my bunk. I'll get up there."
Boy, it tickled him to death. He was a real nice old guy. I guess he's
dead now. Evidently he had a real good spitball at one time.

My first manager was Kid Elberfeld, in the Western Association.
He was old when he managed us. He was a good little manager, but
he was a character. I mean a real character. He called everyone a
"rock head." Kid Elberfeld had the five-daughter basketball team.
They went all over. Nobody could beat 'em. He got quite a few
write-ups about that.

I didn't get to pitch but one or two years against Joe DiMaggio,
but Vince DiMaggio played on our team. But first Vince was with
San Francisco. Vince took Joe to spring training one year, and Joe
beat him out of his job. And then we signed him up. Vince could hit
a ball hard as Joe, maybe harder. But every time he hit a home run,
then he'd strike out about 30 times trying to hit another one. And
when he'd forget about hitting home runs, then he'd hit one. He
could hit a ball as hard as anybody. And he was a good outfielder.
One of the best sun field outfielders I ever saw. He wouldn't lose a
ball in the sun. Some of them guys did. But he had a knack. He had
sunglasses, but he could use his hand and do just as well. He was
with me in San Diego quite a while, and we played together at Pittsburgh. Vince used to come over to the house when we were in San
Diego. We'd play Monopoly at night. He was also quite a singer. Ed
Wells and I lived close together all the time we were in San Diego,
and Ed would tell our wives, "Don't ask Vince to sing! The neigh-
bors are gonna run us out!" He liked to sing opera, and he sang loud
and real high. He had a good voice. You know they wrote a song
about Joe DiMaggio while he was with the Yankees. Well, Vince
used to sing that song. Only he'd use his own name. Vince was a
good guy. In fact all three of them guys were. Dominic, Joe, and
Vince. They were all real nice guys. I really think Vince could cover
more ground out in center field than Joe could.

Sam Gibson pitched a lot of years with Frisco. But Ballou, Old
Ballou, saved all his ball games for him. He used to relieve. They tell
me—I never did see him do this—but they say Old Ballou had a little bottle of liquor there, and whenever O'Doul would flag him and
tell him to come on in, he'd take one good swallow and then walk to

De Maggio Trio

De Maggio Pair May Play for S. F. Ball Club

Oldest Member of Trio Paves Way for His Brothers

Another brother act, which some say parallels the Waner family, is expected to make its bow before San Francisco Seal customers in the 1933 Coast League campaign at the Seals Stadium.

This act, with Vincent and Joe de Maggio playing parts, has won Coast League recognition after classy work in the "bush circuits" and figures to make good on the "big time" here.

Vincent, head man of the act, joined the Seals in the latter part of July, 1932, and in a short time won the favor of the local fans by his fielding and hitting. While with the Tucson club of the Arizona-Texas League, he rang up a string of twenty-six home runs to lead the batsmen.

The other member of the act, Joe, played with the Seals in the final week of 1932 and showed to such good advantage that he was enrolled in Mickey Shader's baseball school and told to report at the Monterey camp in the spring.

Both boys are fairly good hitters and expert fielders. Vincent cavorts around in the outfield, while Joe performs at shortstop. He is figured to give Young Augie Galan a good time this year.

Besides Vincent and Joe there is Tom, oldest member of the family, who played with the Hollywood Stars a few seasons ago. Tom made quite an impression with Manager Oscar Vitt but when he was hurt in training he called it quits for a spell.

When the boys last tabulated their aggregate batting it totaled 1460, which is pretty good.

This trio started playing baseball at Funston field and were members of outstanding championship teams from that section of the city.

The De Maggio family has been going right ahead in the baseball world. Vincent and Joe, outfielder and shortstop, are expected to play for the Seals this season, while Tom, bottom, had a tryout with the Hollywood Stars a few years ago, but because of an injury had to quit baseball for a spell.

Most fans know there were three DiMaggio brothers—Joe, Vince, and Dominic—but there also was Tom, the elder brother who gave up baseball and remained in San Francisco. *(Copyright © The San Francisco Chronicle. Reprinted with permission.)*

the mound. He wouldn't even warm up. He'd go in there and make his eight pitches and start pitching.

He was good. Old Ballou could throw that overhand curveball, and he always had a man or two on base when he went in there, and they couldn't hardly hit it out of the infield. He was one of the best relievers in that Coast League. And I guess he was pretty old when I was out there.

Gibson was older than me too. His knuckles dragged the ground every pitch. His knuckles on his throwing hand would always skin up. I used to hit him good, because I hit down on the ball, and his ball was coming up. I believe I hit him two or three times in the box during my career. I got more hits through the middle than anywhere.

One of the best pitchers in the league was Tony Freitas. Oh, he used to give us a rough time. I never could hit him. That little sucker, he'd get me out easy. And he'd laugh. He'd throw me something funny—he had all kinds of little stuff he'd dish out there. And I had trouble with left-handers anyway. He had all kinds of little old curves and a screwball that would break in on your hands. He'd smile. He knew he had me.

One year I read in the paper where him and some of his buddies—it was during the baseball season—they killed some pheasants around Sacramento, and they got arrested for it. They killed them out of season. I killed a chucker quail one time in San Diego with a baseball. Those suckers were always in there. We'd go out early sometimes, take batting practice, the pitchers would, and the chuckers—there was a pair of them in there once—and I just thought I'd throw at one, and I hit it. Cooked it. It made a nice meal.

We had some good ex-big leaguers in the Coast League. We had some pretty good hitters in that league. Smead Jolley, he could hit the ball hard, especially pulling it in that second base hole. And if Smead got it up in the air, good-bye. He played with us some, but I played against him too. I used to have fun with him. I'd quick pitch him. I'd watch him and wait and then, when he'd go forward, I'd throw. And he couldn't get the bat back, to swing, so he'd nub the ball if he hit it. He used to give me the devil for quick pitching him.

I had a good curveball and a fairly good fastball. We didn't have clocks then. And I had a good change of pace, which got Babe Ruth out. He couldn't handle that slow curve. I pitched three or four games against the Yankees my first year in the big leagues. I know Ruth didn't hit a home run on me, I don't believe. But Lou Gehrig, he hit a couple of line drives. He hit one through the box. If he'd a hit my leg he would have broke it.

Lazzeri was the toughest guy on the Yankee team for me. He was a right-handed hitter. And Al Simmons was the toughest guy with the A's. I didn't know how to pitch against an opposite-field–hitting right-hander, and that's what Al was. He'd step in the bucket, and he'd hit into right field. And I was pitching him right in his wheelhouse. I was pitching outside to him. You know, a left-hander's ball breaks out. I thought since he was standing pretty far from the plate, I could pitch him outside. But he'd step into the ball, you see, and he'd hit that opposite wall. I don't believe he hit a home run, but he hit the devil out of a couple of 'em against that wall in right field.

And old Hornsby, he was my manager the last year I was with the Browns. He was our manager in 1933. If you'd talk baseball, you'd get along with him good. If you changed the subject, he'd move on. Oh, he liked to talk baseball. He was still a playing manager when he managed the Browns. Once in St. Louis he pinch hit for us, and Lefty Gomez threw him a fastball outside, and out of the park it went, and, boom, we beat 'em 3–2. Gomez was invited to a picture show, to get up and talk at a theater, and a guy stood up and asked Gomez what he threw Hornsby. Gomez cussed him out. He didn't like that at all. He had that game won, then Hornsby hit a home run with a man on in the ninth inning. That's tough on a pitcher like that.

We used to have a third baseman who was scared of a ground ball. He used to run up to me and say, "Pitch outside! Pitch outside!" He was a good hitter, but boy, don't hit him a ground ball. His eyes would just about bulge out of his head when somebody'd hit him a ground ball. He played too stiff. He wasn't relaxed. A good fielder is relaxed out there. He could catch that ball on either side, but he was just stiff as a board when a ball was hit at him. It would hit his glove a lot of times and bounce out.

In Detroit I pitched some there, and I'd see Tommy Bridges. He was one of the best pitchers in the league. He didn't look very big, but man, he could throw a curve like nobody could. And he had a good fastball. His curve broke straight down. "Jug handle" the guys called it. I had a good overhand and sidearm, and I threw an underhand curve that went up. That's why Babe Herman never could get a hit off me. And I pitched a lot against him in the Coast League. He was a good hitter, but he couldn't hit that underhand curve. He'd jump all around that plate and take the craziest swings you ever saw.

Yeah, I used to enjoy pitching. I'd be nervous before the game, but after the first pitch, I'd throw good. Most every pitcher's a little nervous before you throw that first ball. And then you settle down. Old Herman Pillette—he used to be our relief pitcher—he'd stay out in the bull pen. He'd say when I'd pitch if I got by that first inning, he'd relax back there and take a nap. He said if they were going to get me, they'd usually get me in the first inning. But I never did have too many bad first innings.

They called me "Lefty" and "Crooked Arm" because a left-hander couldn't throw a straight ball. "Preacher" was a nickname I had from grade school. They call me that yet around here. How'd I get it? When I went to the first grade in Four Wards School in Lake Charles, they called me and my two brothers the "Preacher Brothers." They said we had some funny little hats the first day of school, said they looked like preachers' hats. I don't know what a preacher's hat would look like, do you? But that's what they said. That's where they came up with that name.

They called me *Hee-burt* everywhere but Louisiana. It's *Ay-bare*. The *H* is silent. They called me *Hee-burt* everywhere but in Louisiana, and I didn't play in Louisiana.

Wallace (Wally) Andrew Hebert

Born Aug. 21, 1907, Lake Charles, LA.
Batted left, threw left. Height: 6' 1". Weight: 196 lbs.

Year	Club	League	G	IP	W	L	Pct.	H	SO	BB	ERA
1930	Springfield	Western Assn.	36	251	15	16	.484	265	154	83	…
1931	St. Louis	American	23	103	6	7	.462	128	26	43	5.07
1932	St. Louis	American	35	108	1	12	.077	145	29	45	6.50
1933	St. Louis	American	33	88	4	6	.400	114	19	35	5.32
1934	Hollywood	Pacific Coast	37	170	11	11	.500	200	53	49	4.23
1935	Hollywood*	Pacific Coast	39	219	10	17	.370	276	79	50	4.94
1936	San Diego	Pacific Coast	35	229	18	12	.600	240	87	51	3.03
1937	San Diego	Pacific Coast	39	244	17	14	.549	257	90	42	3.02
1938	San Diego	Pacific Coast	37	243	12	16	.429	244	102	58	3.11
1939	San Diego	Pacific Coast	39	299	20	10	.667	295	104	64	3.13
1940	San Diego	Pacific Coast	38	280	15	18	.455	316	106	100	3.91
1941	San Diego	Pacific Coast	39	279	22	10	.688	294	102	58	3.00
1942	San Diego	Pacific Coast	40	319	22	15	.594	324	125	78	2.37
1943	Pittsburgh	National	34	184	10	11	.476	197	41	45	2.98
	Major League totals—4 years		125	483	21	36	.368	584	115	168	4.63
	Minor League totals—10 years		379	2533	162	139	.538	2711	1002	633	…

*Hollywood franchise transferred to San Diego

13

Chicago's Blazing Shortstop

BILLY JURGES

The book Cult Baseball Players *came out in 1990. Writers and celebrities contributed chapters on various players who at some point had caught their interest. If ever a* Cult Baseball Players II *gets published, I'd like to contribute a chapter on Billy Jurges. It would go something like this. . . .*

Billy Jurges was one of those guys loved by his teammates but despised by the enemy. He played hard. He played rough. He played to win.

Off the field Billy Jurges was a complete gentleman, kind, generous, and self-effacing. But on the field, look out. Billy Jurges was probably the most volatile, out-of-control ballplayer the game has ever seen. He was by no means a villain—just somebody who snapped in the heat of battle and did crazy things.

Like throwing baseballs into the opposing team's dugout. Or slugging an enemy player on behalf of a teammate who had declined a challenge to fight. Then there was the time Billy Jurges punched a former boxer, a man a foot taller than him who, it should be pointed out, was a major league umpire.

The son of a banker, Jurges grew up in a middle-class neighborhood of Brooklyn, where he started playing sandlot ball at age 12, making a name for himself a few years later with a top semipro team called the Hawtree Indians. Because young Bill could cover the ground near shortstop like few others and had a rifle arm, he was offered a contract to play ball. Newark signed him as a 19-year-old in 1927 and assigned him to Manchester, New Hampshire, in the New England League. After two years at Manchester and another two playing for the Reading, Pennsylvania, team in the International League, Jurges was called up by the Chicago Cubs. The rookie played 88 games at shortstop for the Cubs in 1931 but batted poorly, finishing the season with an average of .201.

However, Jurges soon proved he could hit major league pitching and, by the spring of 1932, was established as the shortstop on what is remembered as one of baseball's all-time best infields. At third base was Woody English, a talented player who was moved from shortstop because of the gifted work of Jurges. At second was future Hall of Famer Billy Herman who, like Jurges, was a second-year man in 1932. The first baseman on that stellar infield was the old pro Charlie Grimm. In a few years Grimm and English would be replaced by other standouts, Stan Hack at third base and Phil Cavarretta at first.

In 1932 Jurges's name first appeared in national headlines. It was because of an incident that occured off the field, in a hotel room. Perhaps you know the story. It concerns a young woman and a gun.

Her name was Violet Valli, a pretty brunette who had romantic feelings for Jurges, then 24. Jurges explained to the lovestruck woman, so the story goes, that he wasn't similarly inclined. But over the course of a few months, she grew more and more obsessed with him, calling repeatedly on the telephone with hopes of spending time with the man she felt she loved.

On July 6, 1932, Valli telephoned Jurges at his room in a Chicago hotel. He told her she could come up to talk. According to those who were later interviewed, she brought a gun, which she planned to use on herself. She apparently couldn't foresee any relief from her torment.

When she pulled the gun from her purse, Jurges made a wild lunge and tried to wrestle it from her hand. Three shots were fired. Jurges was shot twice but was not seriously hurt. One bullet tore up the little finger on his left hand, while another struck a rib and ricocheted upward, exiting his body at the right shoulder. Valli was shot through the arm. The incident happened so long ago that it's been all but forgotten, but at the time, very few people in America didn't know the name Billy Jurges and how he nearly lost his life.

In an odd bit of timing, the Jurges story knocked off the front page a baseball feat that should have received a good amount of press, especially in Chicago. On the day that he was shot, Jurges's teammate, the affable Charlie Grimm, became the first player in three years to reach the milestone of 2,000 lifetime hits. When Jurges had recovered and returned to active play, Jolly Cholly no doubt reminded Jurges about what it took to take the attention away from Grimm's accomplishment.

A little over a year later, Jurges again stole a teammate's thunder, but this time it had to do with baseball. The Cubs were in Chicago playing the Philadelphia Phillies in a doubleheader. It was in early September 1933, and the Cubs were fighting tooth and nail, trying to keep alive the possibility of winning a second straight National League pennant. There were some rough plays on the bases, hard slides and things of that nature, and the Philly players, from the dugout, expressed their disapproval of the rough play of the Cubs, especially of shortstop Bill Jurges.

Jurges, hotheaded and short of fuse, picked up a baseball and blazed it into the Philly dugout, scattering the players. He got another ball and fired it too into the dugout. A near player riot was precipitated by Jurges, said the next day's papers. The Philly players swarmed out of the dugout and headed for Jurges, but luckily for everyone involved, especially Jurges, the players were held at bay by Jurges's teammates and a large, tough umpire named George Magerkurth.

There are three punch lines to this story: (1) unbelievably, Jurges was not kicked out of the game; (2) Jurges's antics overshadowed the fact that the Cubs won the game on Dolph Camilli's two-run homer, Camilli's first big league hit; (3) umpire George Magerkurth would, six years later, punch the pesky Bill Jurges. (We'll get to that later.)

As mentioned earlier, Bill Jurges was a favorite of his teammates, but there was at least one exception. Walter Stephenson was a backup catcher on the 1935 Chicago Cubs who one day took off after Jurges with intent to do bodily harm. The fight was broken up in the dugout by Cub manager Charlie Grimm.

Ballplayers call it "giving the needle," a time-honored pastime at which Jurges excelled. But one day he went a little too far with his teammate, Stephenson, a six-foot strongman nicknamed "Tarzan."

Stephenson was a southerner, from North Carolina. During an idle moment in the dugout, Jurges explained that back in Civil War days his grandfather had been a Northern soldier. Somehow, Grandfather Jurges had lost his rifle, but he spotted a large contingent of Confederate soldiers, all well-armed, holed up in a little valley waiting for orders regarding where to go next. Jurges enthusiastically explained that his grandfather picked up a cornstalk, charged the regiment of Confederates, and chased them for a couple of miles, wielding only the cornstalk, which they mistook for a loaded weapon. Jurges told his rapidly boiling teammate that Grandfather Jurges eventually captured the troops. Stephenson sat silently through all of this until Jurges cheerfully added that the prisoners were all from North Carolina, and three of them were named Stephenson. Luckily for Stephenson and Jurges, especially Jurges, the men were quickly separated.

Billy Jurges is remember primarily for the time he spent with the Chicago Cubs—he played in three World Series with them, 1932, 1935, and 1938—but he spent 1939 through 1945 with the New York Giants (before returning to finish his career with the Cubs in 1946 and 1947).

It was while with the Giants in 1939 that Jurges was involved in an imbroglio that has been written about and talked about ever since. The day was July 15, and the Giants were at home playing the Cincinnati Reds at the Polo Grounds.

The Giants were in the field, leading 4–3 in the eighth, with Harry Gumpert on the mound. With a runner on first and Cincinnati outfielder Harry Craft at the plate, Gumpert threw and Craft connected with a long fly ball close to the left-field foul line. It was far enough to be a home run, but the question was, was it a fair ball? Home plate umpire Lee Ballanfant signalled home run, and the situation on the field soon spiraled completely out of control.

Shortstop Billy Jurges pivots and throws to first during a 1938 Cubs-Yankees World Series game. Sliding under Jurges is Joe DiMaggio. (*Courtesy of National Baseball Hall of Fame Library & Archive, Cooperstown, NY*)

The photos from the next day's papers show Giants players, most notably catcher Harry "The Horse" Danning, arguing heatedly with the umpires. Danning was thrown out by Ballanfant, and umpire Ziggy Sears, after listening to Giants outfielder Joe Moore scream for a while, also tossed Moore. Meanwhile, umpire George Magerkurth, a towering, lumbering, former boxer and a presence to be reckoned with, walked slowly toward the plate from his position near first base.

Magerkurth intended to get the game back on track, but he was soon seen jawing hotly with Jurges, who, like all the other Giants players, believed without a doubt that the umpires had blown the call. Jurges and Magerkurth were locked in a rapidly escalating word fight, and then they both snapped. The fans saw Magerkurth throw a jab to Jurges's ribs, and then Jurges, a foot or so shorter than the umpire, jumped and swung a fist at Magerkurth. It wasn't a knockout punch, but Jurges clearly connected.

Jurges, of course, was immediately ejected, and the game eventually was resumed. It ended with the Reds winning, 8–4.

The write-up the next day in *The New York Times* included the following passage—the verbal exchange between Jurges and Magerkurth at its apex:

"Don't you spit in my face," Jurges thundered as he argued with Magerkurth, to which the Major replied, "Don't get your face so near mine and it won't get spit on."

And the next development came when, according to Magerkurth, Jurges roared, "I'll spit in yours."

"I said to him," testified the good Major, " 'I'd like to see you do that,' and so help me, he did. Then he swung and hit me on the cheek."

The upshot was that both Jurges and Magerkurth were fined $150 and suspended for 10 days.

As entertaining and bewildering as the stories about Billy Jurges's exploits are, they unfortunately divert attention from what a truly fine player he was. His career as a major leaguer lasted 17 years. Jurges's reputation, other than for losing his cool, was playing superb defense. A sure-handed, "hit-me-the-ball" in-the-clutch shortstop, he five times led National League shortstops in fielding percentage and was exceptional at turning the double play. He also contributed at the plate. His lifetime batting average was .258, but he hit as high as .298 in 1937 and also once batted .293. His top batting accomplishments were hitting .364 in the 1932 World Series and stroking a near-record nine straight hits for the New York Giants in

1941. Jurges was a gritty ballplayer, no doubt, and except for perhaps 1931 and 1947, the years that bookend his career, he was unquestionably one of the most valuable players on every team for which he played.

After his playing days, Jurges gained quite a reputation as a coach and was respected for sharpening the defensive skills of many young major league infielders, such as the then-struggling Harmon Killebrew. For the Braves he tutored, among others, Johnny Logan and Eddie Mathews.

Jurges, who almost died at 24, lived a long time. He reached the age of 88. He scouted for years and was often given the responsibility of giving the yea or nay on highly praised prospects. Smart baseball men listened to Bill Jurges. He was one of them.

Jurges fought cancer for the last six years of his life. In 1991 he was given a 5 percent chance to live out the year. He wasn't ready to give up. He enjoyed life with his second wife, Phyllis, and wanted to travel with her. He did. He lived until 1997.

Baseball never stopped being important to Billy Jurges. Just before he entered the hospital for the last time, he saw a teenager who he just knew had the tools to make it in baseball. He dictated a letter to his wife, who sent the letter to a general manager Jurges knew. According to Phyllis Jurges, her husband smiled broadly when told the report on the prospect had been received by the baseball executive.

Bill Jurges was, in a word, passionate. He cared. Said Phyllis Jurges, "That man lived and breathed baseball from the time he was a child until the last weeks of his life."

The only reason he stopped working in baseball, at age 75, according to Phyllis Jurges, is that his first wife was dying of cancer. He quit baseball so he could take care of her. Said his widow, Phyllis, who spent 10 years with him, "They didn't come any nicer than Bill Jurges."

Because of his longevity and the fact that he was an eyewitness to one of baseball's most chronicled moments, Billy Jurges was questioned countless times over the years about his opinion on the 1932 Cubs-Yankees World Series game in which Babe Ruth suppos-

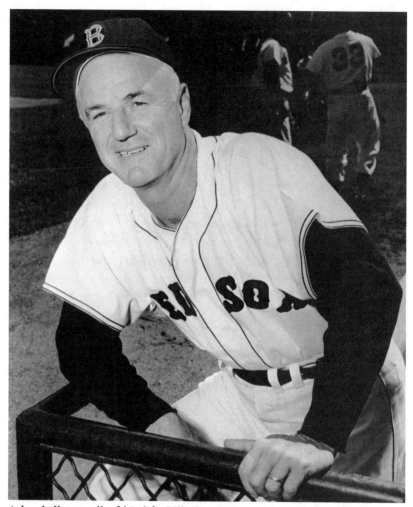

A baseball man all of his life, Billy Jurges managed the Red Sox in 1959 and 1960. (*Courtesy of Boston Red Sox*)

edly signalled that the next pitch offered him would be cranked out of the park.

For those unfamiliar with the circumstances that led up to that moment, here are the details. After being shot by Violet Valli in 1932, Jurges was out of action for three weeks. The Cubs purchased former Yankee shortstop Mark Koenig from the San Francisco Missions to shore up the infield. Koenig played magnificently, helping the Cubs win the pennant, but was voted only a partial share of the World Series money. The Yankees players, led by Ruth, razzed the Cubs incessantly during the World Series because of the shoddy treatment they felt was given their old teammate.

At the height of the hostilities, Ruth supposedly pointed to a spot in the center field bleachers where he planned to deposit the next pitch. Many feel the story is pure bunkum. Certainly the Cubs players always felt that way. Many of the Yankees also indicated the story was fantasy. What Ruth was really doing was raising a finger to indicate he still had one strike left, which made for a pretty dramatic moment in itself. (I personally feel it's the most overblown story in baseball. Even if Ruth was announcing that he expected to launch a home run, is that such an unfathomable concept? We're talking about the greatest home-run hitter in the history of the game.)

Because of the attention given that game, the names of many, including Billy Jurges, will forever be linked to that moment from baseball's past. We're left with a vision of young Billy Jurges, stationed at shortstop, watching helplessly as Ruth's drive rises higher and higher before landing agonizingly, for the Cubs, beyond the outfield wall.

Other images define him better, such as standing at shortstop throwing baseballs into the Philadelphia dugout. Now that's Billy Jurges.

William (Billy) Frederick Jurges

Born May 9, 1908, Bronx, NY. Died March 3, 1997, Clearwater, FL.
Batted right, threw right. Height: 5'11". Weight: 175 lbs.

Year	Club	League	Position	G	AB	R	H	2B	3B	HR	RBI	BA
1931	Chicago	National	2B-3B	88	293	34	59	15	5	0	23	.201
1932	Chicago	National	SS-3B	115	396	40	100	24	4	2	52	.253
1933	Chicago	National	SS	143	487	49	131	17	6	5	50	.269
1934	Chicago	National	SS	100	358	43	88	15	2	8	33	.246
1935	Chicago	National	SS	146	519	69	125	33	1	1	59	.241
1936	Chicago	National	SS	118	429	51	120	25	1	1	42	.280
1937	Chicago	National	SS	129	450	53	134	18	10	1	65	.298
1938	Chicago	National	SS	137	465	53	114	18	3	1	47	.245
1939	New York	National	SS	138	543	84	155	21	11	6	63	.285
1940	New York	National	SS	63	214	23	54	3	3	2	36	.252
1941	New York	National	SS	134	471	50	138	25	2	5	61	.293
1942	New York	National	SS	127	464	45	119	7	1	2	30	.256
1943	New York	National	SS-3B	136	481	46	110	8	2	4	29	.229
1944	New York	National	INF	85	246	28	52	2	1	1	23	.211
1945	New York	National	3B-SS	61	176	22	57	3	3	3	24	.324
1946	Chicago	National	INF	82	221	26	49	9	2	0	17	.222
1947	Chicago	National	SS	14	40	5	8	2	0	1	2	.200
		Major League totals		1816	6253	721	1613	245	55	43	656	.258

World Series Record

Year	Club	League	Position	G	AB	R	H	2B	3B	HR	RBI	BA
1932	Chicago	National	SS	3	11	1	4	1	0	0	1	.364
1935	Chicago	National	SS	6	16	3	4	0	0	0	1	.250
1938	Chicago	National	SS	4	13	0	3	1	0	0	0	.231
		World Series totals		13	40	4	11	2	0	0	2	.275

14

SUPERMAN

ART PENNINGTON

"Why don't you call one of the old Negro League players?" My friend and mentor Peter Golenbock made the suggestion a couple of times. He pointed out that, by including a chapter or two on Negro League players, I could cover ground I hadn't already explored and maybe, if I got lucky, I'd come up with someone noteworthy who'd been forgotten or overlooked.

After doing some research I began focusing on the record of outfielder–first baseman Art Pennington. He had a solid career, but I really didn't know much about him. I was intrigued by his nickname, "Superman," but I liked his regular name even more—for some reason Art Pennington *just sounded like the name of a ballplayer to me.*

I decided for once I'd make a call with little more to go on than a hunch. I got lucky. Art Pennington was fantastic. He definitely gave me more than I bargained for.

ART PENNINGTON: I started with the Ethiopian Clowns. We put on shows for people. We put marks on our face, marked up like Africans and stuff. Zulu Clowns is what it was. That was my first team. It must have been 1938 or 1939. I was young, 15 or 16. My family was real poor in those days, and my aunt sent me five dollars to come over to Memphis. I liked baseball, so I tried out with the Clowns. They hired me and we went all over, barnstorming. It was quite a show. The whole team wore skirts. Grass skirts. It was something. We drew big crowds too. Played the House of David. All those teams.

Then I went with a team called the West Indian Royals. They were supposed to be from the West Indies, but they were mostly Americans; only a few of them were foreigners. So I played with them and then finally I hooked up with the Chicago American Giants in the Black Leagues. That was the Black Major Leagues. They were as good as the majors. We had Satchel Paige, Roy Campanella, Jackie Robinson, Luke Easter. I can name quite a few of them: Buck Leonard, Josh Gibson, Leon Day, Monte Irvin. We had some great players. Quite a few of them are in the Hall of Fame now.

There was a reunion down in Atlanta a couple of years ago. It was "The Black Living Legends of Negro Baseball." It was really nice. They had a big banquet, gave us souvenirs. I'd say there were 75 or 100 ballplayers. Some of those guys I hadn't seen in 40 years, but I recognized them. Some of them were old, crippled. Some of them were blind. Oh, I was glad to see 'em. They all recognized me, 'cause the first thing when I walked in, they called me "Superman." They said, "Why there's Superman."

I grew up in Hot Springs, Arkansas. I played football in Hot Springs at Langston High. I was all-state end there. I was strong. I got the name *Superman* when I was 11 or 12 from my mom. We had an old Essex car and one day we went fishing. The back wheel went flat and we didn't have a jack. So I got some rocks and told Mama, "When I get it high enough, throw these rocks under there." My mother didn't want me to do it; she thought I'd hurt myself, strain myself.

I put my back end against that wheel, and I picked that wheel up high enough for her to put those rocks under it, so the wheel would be off the ground, so we could change it. And Mama said, "Well, my Little Superman."

When I was young I was kind of cocky, because when I got up to bat I used to tell the pitchers to "throw it and duck." If they'd strike me out, I'd come right back and tell 'em, "Throw it and duck." And I would make up. If I hit bad one time, I could come in, hit him the next time.

Art Pennington (*Courtesy of Art Pennington*)

I was a .300 hitter, a switch-hitter. I had more power from the right side. In fact, on my right side I couldn't even bunt. All I could do was swing. My left side, I could guide the ball, bunt, you know, drag it, and I was just a line-drive hitter. But I hit home runs on that right side. That was my power side.

The only man who really made me look bad in baseball was Satchel Paige. I had never met Satchel Paige, he was quite a few years older than me, played against my dad, and we played the Kansas City Monarchs a doubleheader in Detroit. We had 44,000 in the ballpark that day. I hadn't seen my granddaddy since I was eight or nine, and he lived there. So I got my mother and them box seats.

Satchel pitched the first game, and Satchel struck me out three times. I would tell him every time, "Throw it and duck." My manager, Jim Taylor, told me, "Don't feel bad. That's Satchel. He's struck out many." He could throw that ball so hard it looked like it was aspirin. In the second game, the Monarchs pitched a guy named Johnny Markham, one of their aces, and I hit him over that Briggs Stadium in Detroit. Over the top of it. So my granddaddy and all saw me playing. We split the doubleheader, 'cause Satchel beat us, I think 2–0 the first game, and we won the next game, I think 8–5.

I would say we played over 160 games a year, easy. We were playing doubleheaders, sometimes three games a day. We would play a game and never take our uniform off, get in the bus, and just make it to the next town. We'd stop at a store, eat baloney sandwiches, and keep going. I enjoyed it. I had fun. I slept in the bus all the time. I had some nice clothes, and whenever we got to stop in a hotel to take a bath, I'd dress up and go look for the girls.

We'd play everybody. We barnstormed from Mississippi all the way to Canada. All the way to New York.

The American Giants played in Comiskey Park when the White Sox weren't there. And see, if we weren't playing, then the Kansas City Monarchs would come in, and the Memphis Red Sox, and then we would go to Milwaukee. Or we'd go to Philadelphia and play a team there or play the Black Yankees in New York. They had us going around, and we had to play all these little teams, these mixed teams, to make money to keep going. The booking agent had all these towns that had enough people to give the team $500 or $600 to keep going. That's the way it was. But we played many, many games.

The highest money I made with Chicago was $600 a month. That's why I jumped to those foreign clubs like down in Mexico. See, I was making over $5,000 during the summer and, by playing winter ball, I was making almost $8,000. That's why Max Lanier and those major leaguers went to Mexico. 'Cause they were doubling the pay for them. Mickey Owen was making $30,000 in Mexico. And Lanier was making around $30,000. A lot of money. Three of us jumped from the American Giants: Lefty McKinnis, Jesse Douglas, myself. I played on the same team with Sal Maglie. He was tough, and Max Lanier was tough. They were good ballplayers.

That Mexican League was powerful, because they had some of the best colored players, like Ray Dandridge and Wild Bill Wright. Double Duty Radcliffe was there. Leon Day was down there. They had some great ballplayers, I'm telling you.

The most fun I had was in Mexico. When I left this country for the first time in 1945 or 1946, man, when I hit Mexico, I found I could eat anyplace, and I could go anyplace. They had beautiful hotels in Mexico City, as beautiful as Chicago, and I could go out with all different girls: white, black, any kind—any of them you could have. And that was the best of my life. I just couldn't believe it. In fact I didn't want to come back to the United States. But my mother and dad, they kept telling me to come back. So I came back and joined up again with the American Giants.

Then in 1949 the American Giants sold me to Portland in that Coast League. Things weren't too good for me out there. I just couldn't play for the people out there, because they were so prejudiced. See, we went through almost as much stuff as Jackie Robinson. They didn't put black cats on the field like they did Jackie Robinson, but names and things. I wasn't used to that after playing ball in Mexico.

I had married a Spanish girl down there, and she was real white. When I went to Portland we couldn't even stay in the hotel, all that stuff. And the ballplayers' wives didn't want to sit with my wife in the box seats. So I just didn't care to play out there. I had my wife go to New York and send a telegram saying that my kid had an accident. A fellow from Caracas had already contacted me and wanted me to come out there, gonna pay me $3,500 a month, and that was more than I was making anyway. Bill Mulligan, he was a real nice general manager for Portland, he knew how they had mistreated us. So he gave me a ticket to New York. I met my wife in New York, and we flew down to Caracas, Venezuela. And I played there.

I couldn't have gone through what Jackie Robinson went through. I couldn't have took that. No way in the world. Many of those colored players wouldn't have gone through that stuff. See, I was young and cocky, and I was the kind of, you know, you're coming up in the South, and people treated you wrong, you couldn't eat here, and it made me a kind of mean fellow sometimes. That's why I couldn't take it in Portland. I told my wife, "To heck with it. I can't play with these people calling me names." *Black boy* and *chocolate drop* and all this and *coons* and stuff. I said, "How can I play?" I had just come from a free country, Mexico, where I could eat where I wanted, stay in beautiful hotels, and I'm gonna come back to my own country . . . Oh, it was pitiful.

When we first came back from Mexico, we were in Little Rock at the train station. And we went into the colored waiting room. But they didn't want my wife to stay in the colored waiting room, 'cause she was too white. And we couldn't go in the white one. She could go but I couldn't. So we stood out in front of the station.

And when we got back from Cuba, we were in Florida, on a bus, and they were going to stop to eat. But I couldn't go in and eat. That really hurt me. I told my wife to go in there and sit down and get us some coffee and doughnuts, whatever she wanted, and bring me back a couple of hamburgers. She wasn't a citizen yet, but she went right in and sat down. But in my own country, I couldn't even eat. So that made me evil. Very evil.

Oh, I've had a lot of problems. But it's not as bad now. I don't pay it any mind now, because it just don't bother me.

♦ ♦ ♦

I had some good years in baseball, some very good years. In 1958 I played in St. Petersburg, Florida. It was a Yankee farm team. Tommy

Tresh was on that team. We won the championship, first time in 30-some years for that town. I think I hit .338, but some guy beat me out. He hit .339.

I should have gone to the majors the same year as Roger Maris and Bill Tuttle and Harvey Kuenn, about 1953. I beat all those guys out for the batting championship in the Three I League. Played against all those guys, Bill Tuttle, Luis Aparicio. I was the batting champion, and I was supposed to go to St. Louis to play for the Browns. But a lot of bull went on with the St. Louis Browns that year, and I got tired of it. So I jumped and went to the Dominican, to Santo Domingo.

I played in Carthehena, over there in Bukata, where all those dope boys were. Oh, I played in many countries. Winter and summer ball. But my happiest days were in Mexico. I don't let nobody talk bad about Mexico. 'Cause man, I loved Mexico. That was my freedom when I was a young boy.

In 1959 I played for Modesto. That's another Yankee farm team. We won the pennant. I had always said the first year I didn't hit .300 I was going to retire, so I retired after 1959 and went to work at Rockwell-Collins here in Cedar Rapids. They had a ball club, and they hired six baseball players to play on their team. They gave me a job and I played with them. Then after I worked 25 years, I retired. And that was the end of the game.

I was kind of a funny ballplayer. When I was young, the guys would pitch and I would just tell them, "Throw it and duck." Some of those suckers would throw at me too. But I'd tell 'em, "Throw it and duck." Yeah, I was kind of a cocky ballplayer in those days. I was young, and I could run, and I had one of the strongest arms in baseball—you can ask any of the players in the Black Leagues. I could shoot it, I could fire. See, I played all positions. I played short, second, third, all outfield, and when I played short, shoot, they'd hit the ball, and I'd hold it and let 'em run. Pep Young would holler at first base, "Throw it, Supe! Don't hold it." But when I fired, you could hear that mitt pop.

I'm glad they're recognizing the ballplayers from the Black Leagues now, since we're old. I'm younger than a lot of them. I'll be 76 in May. And I'm still in good health. I can dance and I'm about the same as I was maybe 10 years ago. I haven't fallen apart yet.

Art Pennington (*Courtesy of Art Pennington*)

I played in Caracas with Buck Leonard, and I got a picture of that team. About seven of them are gone now. Lot of them are dead. They sent me a list from Kansas City, how many players are gone. But I hope they don't have my name on that list for a good while. The way I feel, I don't think about going now. I'm still looking at the girls. The old lady don't like it, but I still look at 'em. My old lady says, "There's nothing like an old fool." I tell her, "Well, I'm gonna be an old fool. 'Cause I'm enjoying my life."

My wife now, I haven't got my Spanish wife. I'm married to a white girl now. We both worked at Rockwell-Collins. We didn't have any problems. Lot of people didn't like it, but we didn't care.

They all know me around here, because I ran for sheriff of Linn County. And safety commissioner. And mayor. I knew I wasn't going to win, but I just liked to get out there and tell them about the prejudices and stuff. They say I'm outspoken. That's what a lot of them say, but I just never bite my tongue. I went on TV and said they shouldn't just get rid of one of them. I said, "Clean the whole outfit away." Those guys hate to see me talking. But this is a pretty good town.

Yeah, I did everything to let 'em know I was here. I'm happy-go-lucky, just like when I was playing ball. I'm just as happy talking about baseball as playing, and I wish I could go back. Oh, I'd give anything to go back, to 18, and start again. But I don't think they would really like me, because I'd tell the pitchers to "Throw it and duck." That's how good I thought I was in my day.

I should have wrote a book a long time ago because I like to talk about baseball and players I played against. I played against some mighty great ballplayers. One home run I hit, I hit one off of Sal Maglie, but another one I hit that I was real proud of was off Dizzy Dean. I hit Dizzy Dean a many mile. He had the All-Stars playing against the Chicago American Giants, and Dizzy drawed all the people, you know. Oh, a lot of 'em came out to see the star pitcher from St. Louis. Dizzy threw me his fastball, and it left there in a hurry. After the game one of his coaches came up and said, "I'd like to see you hit Dizzy when he was in his prime." And our manager, Jim Taylor—he was an old pro too—he said, "Superman would have hit him if he was in any kind of prime."

And that made me feel real good.

Arthur (Art, Superman) David Pennington

Born May 18, 1923, Memphis, TN.
Batted both, threw right. Height: 5'11". Weight: 185 lbs.

Year	Club	League	Position	G	AB	R	H	2B	3B	HR	RBI	SB	BA
1940	Chicago	NAL	1B–OF	—	—	—	—	—	—	—	—	—	—
1941	Chicago	NAL	1B–OF	—	—	—	—	—	—	—	—	—	—
1942	Chicago	NAL	OF	—	65	—	12	3	—	1	—	0	.185
1943	Chicago	NAL	OF	—	62	—	12	1	3	2	—	1	.194
1944	Chicago	NAL	OF	46	157	35	47	6	3	4	37	4	.299
1945	Chicago	NAL	OF	68	234	48	84	16	1	5	24	18	.359
1946	Chicago	NAL	OF	—	—	—	—	—	—	—	—	—	—
1946	Mont.VC, Puebla	Mexican	1B–OF	80	290	40	91	14	3	5	48	8	.314
1947	Puebla	Mexican	1B–OF	123	437	86	127	10	10	5	50	6	.291
1947–1948	Leones	CWL		—	77	6	18	3	1	0	10	1	.234
1948	Puebla	Mexican	1B–OF	84	276	48	83	18	8	4	42	12	.301
1949	Chicago	NAL	OF	57	201	39	70	—	—	—	—	—	.348
1949	Portland	Pacific Coast	OF	20	53	7	11	1	0	0	2	1	.208
1949	Salem	WINT	OF	18	65	15	20	3	0	2	16	3	.308
1950	Chicago	NAL	OF	43	146	40	54	10	2	6	28	14	.370
1951	Chicago	NAL	OF	—	—	—	—	—	—	—	—	—	—
1952	Keokuk	III	OF	116	427	126	149	17	10	20	89	24	.349
1953	Cibaenas	DMSL	OF	—	48	12	11	—	—	—	12	1	.229
1953	Keokuk, Ced. Rap.	III	OF	64	225	45	74	13	1	4	31	10	.329
1954	Cedar Rapids	III	OF	119	423	88	146	22	6	16	79	11	.345
1958	St. Petersburg	FLST	OF	128	419	94	142	26	7	8	93	12	.339
1959	Modesto	CAL	OF–1B	108	359	62	92	18	5	10	65	14	.256

15

THE FRENCHY
AND VICKI SHOW

FRENCHY BORDAGARAY

*It's an oft-told story, and a good one. After a close play an argument ensued—
a short, fiery player stood toe-to-toe with a massive ump. During the exchange,
the player, nearly frothing at the mouth, accidentally spat on the man in blue.
"You're out of the game!" hollered the ump. And of course he was. Later, the
league president levied a sizable fine and suspended the guilty party. The player
exclaimed, "Maybe I did wrong. But the penalty was a little more than I expec-
torated." The classic quote was authored by a former Brooklyn Dodger, a likable
outfielder–third baseman named Stanley George "Frenchy" Bordagaray.*

*Those who recall Frenchy Bordagaray remember him as one of the colorful
misfits who played for the Dodgers during an era when "Dem Bums" won
hearts but not many games. Casey Stengel was the manager for much of that
time, and Frenchy Bordagaray was known to make Casey shake his head—but
also grin. Grin or grimace. It was always one or the other with Frenchy. Branch
Rickey said this about Bordagaray in 1938, when Rickey was the Cardinals'
general manager and Frenchy was the team's third baseman. "He's either the
greatest rotten third baseman in baseball or the rottenest great third baseman.
But he's never in between."*

◆ ◆ ◆

In January of 1996 I was driving back to San Francisco after spending a couple of days with a friend and his family in L.A. I stopped in Ventura and had a late breakfast at a place called Franky's, and while there I remembered that Ventura was the residence of Frenchy Bordagaray. I'd researched Bordagaray's career, and to be honest, I don't know why I hadn't contacted him before. I certainly had thought about it. All the information I'd come across pointed to Frenchy being a character. I was sure he'd be fun to talk with.

After I left the restaurant I checked a phone book and found he was listed. I phoned and, when he invited me over, I, of course, was delighted.

I hopped in my car and a few minutes later I was greeted at the front door by Frenchy and his wife, Vicki, at an Ozzie and Harriet *house in a* Leave It to Beaver *neighborhood a little north and east of central Ventura.*

Frenchy was short, maybe five-foot-six. He looked a few years younger than his 86 years, but not much. His viselike handshake was hard to ignore. Same for the Gene Baker Band-Aid across his nose. I was impressed with his wife's personality. She's a pistol. Together they're two alternating six-shooters busting up the joint. In other words, they're a delightful couple.

◆ ◆ ◆

"All the stories about me are true," said Frenchy Bordagaray. Three chairs were drawn close together. We were sitting in a cluttered but comfortable den. Soft sunlight came in through the sliding glass doors. I told Frenchy there was a question I'd been anxious to ask him. "You want to know about the expectorating story?" he said. I said it was something else. I'd once come across a humorous write-up of a game in Sacramento, and Frenchy was the center of the story. The headline read, "Sacramento Player Forgets He's in Game." Apparently Frenchy forgot to come out to his position in right field at the start of the ninth inning in a game against Portland. The pitcher threw the ball, and the batter slapped the pitch into right field. It was only then that the players and fans realized something was amiss. The center fielder retrieved the ball and threw it in while the batter motored into second with a stand-up double. How a player could forget he was in a game was beyond me. I hoped Frenchy wouldn't be embarrassed by my asking about it. I soon realized I needn't have worried.

FRENCHY: Yes, I remember that. That's a true story.

VICKI: He was sitting on the john.

Stanley "Frenchy" Bordagaray and his wife, Vicki, at a 1946 banquet in Quebec, Canada, celebrating Frenchy's successful first season as a manager. Bordagaray led the Trois Rivières Royals of the Canadian-American League to victory in a tightly contested pennant race, aided in part by standout players Roy Partlow, one of the first blacks in organized baseball, and Frenchy himself, whose .363 average led the league. (*Courtesy of Vicki Bordagaray*)

FRENCHY: I was sitting on the john, yeah. Earl McNeely was our manager. I had to go to the toilet. I went to the toilet and I was a little late coming out. When I came out the guy hit the ball already. He hit it into right field and there was nobody in right field. I was the right fielder. Nobody noticed it.

VICKI: That's why the manager gave the pitcher that warning, "Whenever you're going to pitch look to see that everybody's on the field."

FRENCHY: They blamed the pitcher for it. McNeely gave him hell for pitching the ball. He said, "Don't you look to see that your players are all in position?" He said, "I usually do, but I didn't this time." They didn't bawl me out for it.

VICKI: There was a time under Casey Stengel, this was in the early '30s, what was it, you were at second base and you were supposed to slide into third base, but you didn't. Casey said, "I'm gonna fine you 50 bucks for that." And the next day he hit a home run and, to show Casey up, he slid into first base, second base, third base, and home plate, and Casey said, "It's gonna cost you another 100 bucks for showing me up."

FRENCHY: It happened when I was in Brooklyn. Playing against the Giants. Imagine. Playing the Giants. They were our worst enemies. It was in all the papers.

VICKI: Stan received his award at Brooklyn this year. He told that story to the crowd. They just roared. He said it to the audience when he was admitted to the Brooklyn Hall of Fame. He did some crazy things. That's because he's kooky. He's been beaned so many times.

FRENCHY: I've been hit in the head four times.

VICKI: Six times. The last time they gave him last rites at home plate. He was beaned and the ball went right back to the pitcher.

FRENCHY: Line drive to the pitcher.

VICKI: That poor kid, he couldn't pitch after that. He was shaking like a leaf. This was back in the '40s. With the Dodgers. '43 or '44.

FRENCHY: So many things happened to me. Just like I was telling someone, who was that guy, that outfielder, black guy . . .

VICKI: Oh, Reggie Jackson.

FRENCHY: Reggie Jackson. He said he was the first player with a mustache . . .

VICKI: . . . in the 20th century. But Stan was. You should have heard him.

FRENCHY: That stinker saying he was the first guy. He wants so much glory, let him have it.

VICKI: The Oakland A's had a mustache day, so Stan went up there.

FRENCHY: It was a nice ceremony. The owner called me up and asked me to come up there and be the master of ceremonies, so I went.

VICKI: Reggie was on the team then.

FRENCHY: He was on the team then. They won the pennant that year. When I went there Reggie Jackson was chasing flies in the outfield before the game. He came in and he saw me. He said, "Are you Frenchy Bordagaray?" I said, "Yes." I shook his hand and made him go down to his knees. He said, "My god, I can sure tell you're an old-time ballplayer."

Frenchy then talked about helping Hank Greenberg learn how to play the outfield and Vicki mentioned how Frenchy and Pepper Martin demonstrated sliding techniques to their St. Louis Cardinal teammates in spring training. Then Vicki remembered a story.

VICKI: Stan was on second base and Casey Stengel was the manager. I think it was against the Giants. He was at second base tapping his foot, not paying attention, and they threw the fielder the ball and tagged him out. Stan came in from second base, back to the bench. Casey starts to make a fight with the umpire. "What are you putting him out for? He was on second base." So Stan says, "Leave him alone, Casey. He caught me between taps."

FRENCHY: I've got a lot of stories. I went into third base one day, and Casey said, "Why didn't you slide?" I said, "I couldn't slide. I had tobacco in my back pocket." You know what I did one time? The last game of the season, we were playing the Giants, and a guy hit a fly ball. I was playing left field. I went to catch the ball and my hat flew off. I went back and got my hat and put it on, and I went and caught the ball.

VICKI: The whole crowd in the stadium went, "Ooooh." That's a true story.

FRENCHY: The ball went sky-high. If it was a line drive, heck, I couldn't do it.

VICKI: When they print that story they never finish it. After he went back to get his cap he caught the ball.

I asked Vicki if they were married at the time. "No," she told me. "We were married in '41." Frenchy came up to the big leagues in 1934 with the Chicago White Sox. He had two tours of duty with the Dodgers, 1935–36 and 1942–45.

FRENCHY: I hit Casey Stengel in the ear one time. I was warming up with Joe Stripp. I was wild anyhow. When I played third base I used to throw 'em in the bleachers. Anyhow, I cut loose with Joe Stripp, and he jumped up and he couldn't get it. This was in Cincinnati. Casey was going to hit infield, so he had a bat, and he was yelling his head off. Then when I hit him, he went down. I went to the outfield then, to get the hell out of there. So when he came to—they carried him to the dugout—Casey said, "Who threw that ball!" And Stripp said, "Freeencheee, Freeenchee did it." It was funny, really, the way it turned out.

VICKI: What did Casey say?

FRENCHY: "I'll send Frenchy to Podunk tomorrow!"

I asked Frenchy about the teams he played for.

FRENCHY: I played for Cincinnati in 1939. I pinch ran for Ernie Lombardi in the World Series. Then the Yankees bought me. They had me playing in Kansas City in 1940. I hit .358 there—with Gerry Priddy and Phil Rizzuto. Then I played with the Yankees in 1941. You know how I got off that ball club? Joe McCarthy was the manager. We won the World Series. I told McCarthy, "If Casey Stengel had as many good ballplayers as you had he would have won 20 championships." Casey almost did, too, when he took over the Yankees.

VICKI: Stan told McCarthy this when they were celebrating the championship. They'd played the Dodgers and they were celebrating. See, he was kind of loaded a little bit.

FRENCHY: I was loaded and Casey was sitting next to McCarthy, and I said, "This guy here, if he had . . ."

Stanley George "Frenchy" Bordagaray, a .283 lifetime hitter, was one of base-ball's best pinch hitters. His career pinch-hitting average of .312 is second all time (minimum 150 at bats), behind Tommy Davis's .320. In 1938 Bordagaray had perhaps the finest pinch-hitting season in history, connecting 20 times in 43 at bats as a member of the St. Louis Cardinals. (© *Brace Photo*)

VICKI: And Casey was going, "Shhhh, shhh."

FRENCHY: Casey was trying to get me to be quiet. But I was about half swacked. The whole club was swacked.

VICKI: Stan played with the Gas House Gang. You hear about Pepper Martin and the Mudcat Band? They made more money playing music than playing baseball.

Frenchy had a photo in his hand. He gazed at it and said, "This guy, he's a nice looking man." I looked over and saw Frenchy was admiring a picture of Frenchy Bordagaray. Frenchy grinned and Vicki rolled her eyes. She said Frenchy came from a family of fun-loving people. "The whole family is like that," she said. "We'd sit there and laugh about everything. They told the cutest stories. One after another. His father was a darling."

Frenchy told about growing up in Coalinga and being admitted to nearby Fresno State College on an athletic scholarship. The name he made for himself as a track star and halfback on the football team led to his getting a tryout with Sacramento in the Pacific Coast League in 1931.

FRENCHY: My father was a bootlegger. But I loved him anyway. I don't mind telling people about it. But when I was a kid I used to walk through the alleys because I was ashamed. He was a bootlegger, but that's nothing. He had seven kids to raise. That's the reason he did it. He didn't want his kids to starve. I was still proud of him. He was a good athlete too.

Frenchy mentioned receiving a letter recently from four men in prison. He had sent them all autographs. "But," he quipped, "I hope they don't come and look me up." Vicki Bordagaray quietly walked to a nearby desk, leafed through some papers, and found the letter. The short note said,

> I'm a 23-year-old serving time in prison for a mistake I made as a teenager. A few weeks ago some fellow inmates and myself started collecting baseball autographs as a way to keep out of trouble and finally get some mail. Mr. Bordagaray, because of our ages we have never seen you play, but it will be an honor to receive your autograph. Will you please sign these index cards for us? What teams did you play with? Thank you.

Vicki handed me a three-by-five card with a photo of Frenchy in a Yankee uniform. She gave it to me as a gift and said they had sent one just like it to each of the pris-

oners. I thanked her but couldn't resist saying I might want to draw a mustache on it. The card was autographed by Frenchy, which pleased me. I admitted I'd never been an autograph collector. Said Frenchy, "Well, you are now."

FRENCHY: I had five brothers and we were all called Frenchy. But I'm not a Frenchman. I'm a Basque. Nobody ever got that right.

VICKI: You can quote me. When I'm mad at him I call him "a son of a Basque."

FRENCHY: My father came to this country when he was 15 years old.

VICKI: His father was a sheepherder.

FRENCHY: He said he cried every night his first year over here. My mother was born in Merced. She was French. The Basque people speak three languages: Spanish, French, and English.

VICKI: And Basque.

FRENCHY: And Basque, yeah. It's a tough language to learn. There's 1,500 Japanese words in the Basque language. But we're not Asian. The Basque live between France and Spain in the Pyrenees Mountains. But they don't know where they came from.

VICKI: They think they came from Atlantis.

"So that's who I'm interviewing," I said. "The man from Atlantis." I'd learned when I was a kid that Atlantis was a mythical continent. But after talking to Frenchy and Vicki Bordagaray for a while, I was ready to believe differently. Then they informed me that the game of jai alai was brought to America by Basque sailors who jumped ship during Columbus's voyage to the New World. After that Vicki told me a couple of cute tidbits about their children, and they talked about an as-yet unpublished book about Frenchy written by a former sportswriter. I was interested in all that the two told me, including the stories about their family and the fact that Bordagaray means "house on the hill." Even the bandage on Frenchy's nose had significance. It made it easier for him to breathe, he volunteered, and since I've had similar difficulties during sleep, I paid attention to his explanation and gladly accepted the container of bandages he offered me when our visit ended.

I don't know what I can say about the Bordagarays. Great couple, unique, down-to-earth. I won't forget them.

Stanley George (Frenchy) Bordagaray

Born January 3, 1910, Coalinga, CA.
Batted right, threw right. Height: 5' 7½". Weight: 175 lbs.

Year	Club	League	Position	G	AB	R	H	2B	3B	HR	RBI	BA
1931	Sacramento	Pacific Coast	OF	70	252	35	94	19	4	5	32	.373
1932	Sacramento	Pacific Coast	OF	173	692	131	223	33	10	5	77	.322
1933	Sacramento	Pacific Coast	OF	117	416	67	146	26	3	7	65	.351
1934	Chicago	American	OF	29	87	12	28	3	1	0	2	.322
1934	Sacramento	Pacific Coast	OF	117	483	84	155	34	1	6	46	.321
1935	Brooklyn	National	OF	120	422	69	199	19	6	1	39	.282
1936	Brooklyn	National	2B-OF	125	372	63	117	21	3	4	31	.315
1937	St. Louis	National	3B-OF	96	300	43	88	11	4	1	37	.293
1938	St. Louis	National	OF	81	156	19	44	5	1	0	21	.282
1939	Cincinnati	National	OF	63	122	19	24	5	1	0	12	.197
1940	Kansas City	American Association	OF	154	598	113	214	39	8	4	83	.358
1941	New York	American	OF	36	73	10	19	1	0	0	4	.260
1942	Brooklyn	National	OF	48	58	11	14	2	0	0	5	.241
1943	Brooklyn	National	3B-OF	89	268	47	81	18	2	0	19	.302
1944	Brooklyn	National	3B-OF	130	501	85	141	26	4	6	51	.281
1945	Brooklyn	National	3B-OF	113	273	32	70	9	6	2	49	.256
1946	Trois Rivières	Canadian-American	Mgr	104	353	78	128	27	7	4	83	.363
1947	Greenville	South Atlantic	Mgr	48	152	33	52	8	5	1	35	.342
		Major League totals		930	2632	410	745	120	28	14	270	.283
		Minor League totals		783	2946	541	1012	186	38	32	421	.344

World Series Record

Year	Club	League	G	AB	R	H	2B	3B	HR	RBI	BA
1939	Cincinnati	National	2	0	0	0	0	0	0	0	.000
1941	New York	American	1	0	0	0	0	0	0	0	.000
		World Series totals	3	0	0	0	0	0	0	0	.000

16

Short Stories

Remembering Hack:
Les Munns

A native of St. Paul, Minnesota, Les Munns pitched for the Brooklyn Dodgers and St. Louis Cardinals in the 1930s and later played semipro ball in Oklahoma and Georgia. Here's what he remembers about Hack Wilson, the muscle-bound slugger who knocked in 190 runs in 1930.

LES MUNNS: Hack Wilson was with us in Brooklyn in '34. I think they kept him for about six weeks, something like that. He got so he just couldn't see. He'd take strikes, and he'd swear they were outside, and they'd check it out and find the ball was over the plate, so the Dodgers let him go. His vision got where it was bad. But I'll tell you, he was a good ballplayer. I guess the news media didn't care too much about him. That's why it took so long for him to get in the Hall of Fame.

He was built like a hydrant. He had small ankles, and he used about a roll of tape on each ankle, every day. Because if he rounded first base or second like that, without tape on, he'd roll it. He'd sprain his ankles. He was barrel chested. He hit home runs in every right field in the National League, and he was a right-handed hitter. He used a bat just about as big around as your thumb, you know, down on the handle. And boy, he'd get out in front. I'd pitch batting

189

Hack Wilson (*Courtesy of National Baseball Hall of Fame Library & Archive, Cooperstown, NY*)

practice to him like that, and you'd pitch him inside, deliberately, and he'd hit line drives out to right field. How he ever hit it I don't know.

One Colorful Character: Virgil Trucks

In 1992 I talked with Virgil Trucks via telephone and set up an interview between the former pitcher and Jack B. Moore. Remembered as one of the top American League pitchers of the 1940s and '50s, Trucks is also known for his yarn-spinning ability. Here are two of the stories Trucks told Moore. One is a revealing glimpse into the personality of Mickey Mantle. (Trucks was interviewed before Mantle passed away.) But first, Virgil Trucks gives a fanciful account of how he got started in pro ball.

VIRGIL TRUCKS: That happened as you know when I was a kid going to school, walking like three miles a day to the school and back, down a railroad track. There were a lot of nice rocks on those railroad tracks that just fit into your hand perfectly to throw. One day after I had come home my dad sent me out to get some squirrels for dinner, and so I got my little bag of rocks and went into the woods, and I'm down there throwing and knocking these squirrels one right after the other out of the trees with the rocks and picking them up and putting them in my bag to take home. And this scout—I don't know how this scout happened to be in the area but he was, and he saw me do this. He came out of nowhere, and he asked me my name and I told him, and then he said, "Where do you live?" And I told him over that little hill there. And he said, "Will you introduce me to your father?" And I said, "Sure, come on home with me."

So we walked home and I introduced my dad to this scout and the scout tells my dad, "Mr. Trucks," he says, "I can make him the greatest southpaw that ever pitched in the major leagues." And my dad says, "Well, he's not a southpaw. He's right-handed."

And the scout said, "Well, I just saw him down in those woods knocking those squirrels out of the trees one right after another left-handed and knocking them out just as accurate as you please."

And my dad said, "Well, the reason he throws left-handed at the squirrels is because if he throws right-handed he mangles them up so bad we can't eat 'em."

◆ ◆ ◆

VIRGIL TRUCKS: Mickey Mantle and I are very close friends. Always have been, even when we were competitors against one another. And then when I finished up with the Yankees I played with them for that final year, and Mick and I became very close friends. I've been to a lot of golf tournaments where he played, and in fact he had his own golf tournament named after him, in Chattanooga, Tennessee. So me living in Birmingham, 150 miles away, he would always invite me to play in his tournament. So I did for several years, and then one year I had one named in my honor in Birmingham, and I called him. He was living in New York or going between New York and Dallas where his home is, and I called him in New York 'cause I knew he was there, and I asked him if he would come play in my tournament, and he said, "Sure, tell me when it is." So I told him and he flew into Birmingham, and I picked him up at the airport and took him out to my house and we had a little cookout the night before the tournament. When we finished dinner, my wife said, "Mick, how about writing something on this stairwell wall here going down into the basement." He said OK. It's just a regular white wall going down there, and we gave him a big marking pencil and he went down on the top step and wrote, "To Ethel and Virgil, thank you for having me in your home, and don't paint over this, you assholes," signed "Mickey Mantle." We almost fell down the stairs laughing when he finished with it.

So later on we moved from this house and I had a guy out looking at the house and of course we showed him that and he was sort of a baseball fan anyway, a franchise dealer for Domino's Pizza. He was the one buying our house, and I said, "We'll paint over that thing and nobody will see it." And he said, "If you paint over it, I won't buy the house."

The Walking Machine:
Pete Hughes

A .300 hitter is considered a valuable offensive commodity, but it should be remembered that a player who walks frequently also contributes to his team's offense. Eddie Lake, for instance, batted only .211 in 1947, but consider his 120 walks and you can see why Lake was able to score 96 runs that year.

Ted Williams had the highest lifetime walking average, .208, with the runner-up being Max "Camera Eye" Bishop at .204. Sadaharu Oh, who led the Japanese Central League in walks 16 consecutive years, is the Japanese record holder with a walking average of .205.

But a forgotten minor league player named Gabriel "Pete" Hughes compiled the highest walking average, .271, of any professional ballplayer. He played from 1937 through 1952 (losing 1942–45 to the service) and led his league in walks 9 of his last 10 years, with a high of 210 in 1949. A lifetime .350 hitter, he also had power, leading four minor leagues in home runs.

A teammate of Hughes in 1939 at Ogden in the Pioneer League was Bobby Adams, who was starting a career in baseball that lasted over 50 years. Adams, who certainly knew his baseball, once said, "Pete Hughes was one of the finest hitters I've ever seen. At any level."

Pete Hughes never played anywhere but in the low minors, and with the aid of another of his 1939 Ogden teammates, Pete Deas, we'll shed a little light on the pluses and minuses of the talents of one of the minor leagues' most intriguing players.

WALTER "PETE" DEAS: I knew Pete Hughes well. He played with me on the Ogden club. I think he hit about 42 or 43 home runs that year. Jeez, he could hit. I saw him hit a ball in Salt Lake City. The pitcher ducked it was hit so low. But it must have gone over 400 feet. It looked like a shooting rocket. It just kept going, higher and higher. I might be exaggerating a little, but I don't think so. It looked to me like it cleared the fence by about a hundred feet.

Pete Hughes always had a smile on his face. He liked to laugh. The only thing he didn't like was left-handed pitchers. He hated them. He used to holler at us, "Get this guy out of the pitcher's box, quick."

He was duckfooted, couldn't run. He must have broken both his legs or something. You could never do anything with him when he was on base. You couldn't hit and run or have him go from first to third. It had to be hit out of the park. I may be exaggerating, but he was slow.

He was an outfielder, played right field. He had a pretty good arm, but he wasn't too good a fielder. He couldn't cover a lot of ground. When I went to the East Texas League the next year I lost track of him. He was a good person. Pete Hughes, that guy could hit.

In the dugout with the 1939 Odgen Reds: (left to right) Wes Deardon, Pete Deas, Chet Rosenlund, Billy Hebert, Pete Hughes, Bobby Adams, Lindy Serpa, and Dick Adams. Slugger Pete Hughes, a .350 lifetime hitter in the minors, walked more often than any other player in baseball history, including a staggering 210 times in 1949. Bobby Adams and his brother Dick later reached the majors, while Billy Hebert died in his 20s while serving in the armed forces during World War II. The Stockton, California, ballpark is named in his honor. (*Courtesy of Walter "Pete" Deas*)

Bobby Adams's brother Dick put it plainly why Pete Hughes walked so much: "Sure, 'cause they wouldn't pitch to him."

The Last of the '27 Yanks: Mark Koenig

I was hitchhiking through Northern California in 1971 or 1972, and a carload of people stopped. They were going to the beach and invited me along. But they needed to pick up some things at their place first. We drove down winding, tree-lined Warm Springs Road in the cozy town of Glen Ellen, and I noticed that the mailbox for the house next to where we stopped said, "Koenig." I mentioned the name Mark Koenig, the former Yankee shortstop, not really expecting a reaction. I was surprised to hear, "That's him. He lives there." They were surprised I had heard of him.

I rang the bell and up to the screen door walked a fairly old man with a square face and eyebrows gone to seed. Koenig and I talked for about 15 minutes, and about a year later while on a long bike ride I passed through Glen Ellen and gave him a call. "Come on over," he said.

A tough old bird, Koenig had a lot of emotion in his voice. He would get agitated when he talked about the failure of the pension fund to help out the old ballplayers or about the Cubs not giving him a full World Series share after he helped them to the 1932 pennant. "I blame that Wrigley," Koenig told me. "He should have done something about it." (Philip K. Wrigley was the Cubs' owner.)

I was amazed to discover that when Babe Ruth belted his record-setting 60th home run in 1927, my new friend with the bushy eyebrows had witnessed the blow while leading off third base (after tripling). He mentioned keeping in touch with former teammates Joe Dugan, George Pipgras, Henry Johnson, and Waite Hoyt. He talked about playing for Cincinnati when that team became the first major league team to travel by plane, although he and Jim Bottomley, nervous about air travel, continued to get around by train.

When I told Koenig I would be playing softball later that evening, he mentioned going into Canada once on a hunting trip with a group of ballplayers and being challenged by a local softball team. He laughed and added that, much to their chagrin, the major leaguers were trounced. When I left for my game, he said, "Tell them you were out talking to an old shortstop."

Before he died in 1993, Koenig was the last remaining member of the fabled 1927 Yankees. Koenig appeared in five World Series, leading all hitters in the 1927 classic with a batting average of .500. The 1926 World Series was Koenig's first, and he was on hand to see ancient Grover Cleveland Alexander come out of the bull pen in the seventh game to strike out Tony Lazzeri with the bases loaded.

The last time I talked with Koenig I interviewed him for an article I hoped to sell to Baseball Digest. *As it happened,* Baseball Digest *had just accepted an article on Koenig by another writer and mine never ran. These quotes from Koenig have never before appeared in print.*

MARK KOENIG: Yes. Sure. I was in that game when Alexander struck out Lazzeri. He struck him out on a bad ball. It was a curveball that was outside. On the pitch before that Lazzeri hit a line drive down the left field line, but it was foul. It would have been a home run if it was fair. That was a ball game we should have won. Bob Meusel

Mark Koenig (*Courtesy of National Baseball Hall of Fame Library & Archive, Coop-erstown, NY*)

dropped a fly ball and I gummed up a double play. They beat us four games to three.

Babe Ruth and I had a little altercation in Baltimore during an exhibition game in 1927. He was playing first base this game, and there was a ball hit to Lazzeri. It was a double-play ball and Lazzeri threw the ball about 10 feet over my head. I didn't even make an attempt for it, and Ruth started in saying, calling me every kind of a dumb bum. So I waited until everything was quiet, and I called him a big yellow bum. Then when we retired the side, I was the second hitter, Combs was leading off, and I was bent over picking up a bat, and Ruth pushed me from behind, down into the dugout. There were no punches thrown or anything. I used to have the locker next to Ruth, and on the train I had the berth across from him. I didn't talk to Ruth for the rest of the season, until we clinched the pennant. Then we shook hands and said let's forget it.

My strengths? I guess my arm. I had a powerful arm. I was a fair hitter. I hit both ways, right and left. I got my base hits. A couple of times I hit .300, but .279, .280 was about my speed. I was more of a singles, doubles hitter; I never hit many home runs. I was a good fielder, but I had small hands. I made quite a few errors. They weren't throwing errors, they were just balls that I bobbled.

I retired in '37. My back was bothering me, my eyes were going haywire. I had an offer to play with a lumber company up north. They had ballparks, up in northern California. But I never played again. I wanted to be remembered as a good ballplayer.

Alexander's Roommate: Art "Butch" Weis

I knew Art Weis was old, but I didn't know he was deaf. When I called him in 1994 I asked for him by his nickname "Butch." His wife answered, and I heard her tell him I might be an old teammate. I felt bad when I heard that, because I knew there couldn't have been many of them left, and he would be disappointed to find a stranger on the other end of the phone. Weis was 91. He was very gracious, but his lack of hearing made our conversation all but impossible. I didn't know whether he'd recall anything about Grover Cleveland Alexander, who was his teammate on the Cubs from 1922 through 1926, but when I shouted Alexander's name into the phone just about as loud as I could, the two-time minor league batting champion gave a response to prove that baseball makes for extremely mismatched bedfellows.

ART WEIS: Alexander? He was my roommate. We roomed together for years with the Cubs. Of course he never was around the room, because he was out drinking all the time. I used to have to put him to bed every night. When I signed I was a nice clean boy. I drank my ice cream sodas and so forth. I didn't go for that beer and whiskey and wine, stuff like that. I lived a clean, enjoyable life. I enjoyed baseball so much that I didn't care for that junk.

Fired for Striking Out the Babe: Jimmy Zinn Sr.

When Joe DiMaggio first joined the San Francisco Seals, Jimmy Zinn Sr. was one of the team's star pitchers. Zinn, who won nearly 300 minor league games, was also an outstanding hitter, batting .300 lifetime.

JIMMY ZINN JR.: Dad taught Joe DiMaggio how to play the outfield. He and Jerry Donovan got Joe out and taught him how to play the outfield. 'Cause Joe had started as a shortstop. He was just not an infielder. He was made for the outfield. And I was out there. I remember being out there myself when Dad was showing Joe how to go back on a ball and take his eye off of it and go to a spot and turn around and catch it. Joe happened to have that ability. Dad could do it too. Dad played a lot of outfield when he wasn't pitching. And he was a good hitter. If I could've hit like him, I'd a made the major leagues.

Dad would have probably stayed in the major leagues and done well had he not gotten on the wrong side of George Gibson, his manager at Pittsburgh. When he first went up there as a rookie, well, he was doing well in the Texas League. Had a hell of a record. He came back from France and went with the Athletics. And Connie Mack wanted to sign him for $275 a month. And Dad said, "I can make more than that down in the Texas League." So he went back to the Texas League, and then the Pittsburgh Pirates bought him.

When he first got up there with 'em they were playing an exhibition game against the Yankees. And Dad was striking out Babe Ruth and making him look like a monkey out there. Finally Gibson told him to let the Babe hit one. That's what the people were out there to see. And Dad said, "Well, hell, if the fans want a home run I'll hit one myself." And he went up there and hit one over the fence.

But it was about a foot or so foul. And it pissed old George Gibson off. He ordered Dad to let the Babe hit one. And that went against Dad's grain. Because he never was one to give something up like that. He always played to win. So he went out there and let the Babe hit one. He kept fouling them off, fouling them off, and fouling them off, and finally he just threw one down the middle—batting practice speed—and he said the Babe hit one farther than he ever saw one hit in his life. Well he and Gibson never got along after that, and Gibson never really gave him a chance. I didn't only get this story from Dad, but I got it from the *Cleveland Plain Dealer*. "Jimmy Zinn Loses Job," or, "Jimmy Zinn Strikes Out Babe Ruth, Loses His Job." That was the headline. Rogers Hornsby told me about it too. Finally it got to the point where they couldn't stand each other, and Dad just told him, "Get rid of me. Send me anywhere, but anywhere near you." So they sold him to Kansas City. He was a 27-game winner. And a good hitter. And played the outfield. He was a valuable man.

He started managing in '37 at El Paso. I was 13 going on 14, and I went out and played shortstop. And second base. During batting practice, what have you. And scouts would come through and always think that I was showing pretty good promise. Then in '42, early in '43, the Yankees offered me a $10,000 bonus to sign. The scout had gotten authority. A $10,000 bonus was unheard of in those days. But my draft notice came at the same time. A day or two apart. I mean, it just broke my heart. Then after I spent three seasons away from baseball, when I didn't even touch a baseball during World War II, I came back and I was a dink hitter. I never did get my good timing back. I played second base in the minors for seven years. In seven years I hit seven home runs. And all of 'em except one were inside the park home runs.

I finally hit one out my last year. I didn't think it was going out of the park, and I was ripping for two or three. It was one of the best balls I ever hit in my life, and I wasn't even watching it. I took off, and I was between first and second, and I saw the umpire throw his hand up. And I said, "No, he couldn't have caught it!" I mean, I just knew in my mind the guy couldn't have caught the ball. And then the umpire said, "No! It's over the fence!" And I didn't even really get slowed down to a home run trot. I went around those bases on cloud nine.

Gabriel (Pete) Hughes

Born April 16, 1915, Hurley, NM.
Batted left, threw left. Height: 5'11½". Weight: 195 lbs.

Year	Club	League	Position	G	AB	R	H	2B	3B	HR	RBI	BB	BA
1937	DeLand	Florida State	OF	86	297	63	97	18	3	8	71	73	.327
1938	Muskogee	West.A.	OF	8	28	6	7	2	1	2	6	10	.250
1939	Ogden	Pioneer	OF	122	477	140	195	40	5	41	133	101*	.409*
1940	Ogden/Twin Falls	Pioneer	OF	130	471	113	147	30	11	20	112	129*	.312
1941	Spokane	W.Int.	OF	134	466	139*	148	23	4	34*	125	156*	.318
1942-45								(military service)					
1946	Victoria	W.Int.	OF	119	364	109	124	25	1	30	121	132*	.341
1947	Phoenix	Ariz.-Tex.	OF	133	442	180*	164	36	8	38*	167	193*	.371
1948	Phoenix	Ariz.-Tex.	OF	132	415	142	144	38	5	21	118	207*	.347
1949	Las Vegas	Sunset	OF	123	408	156*	143	31	9	24*	126	210*	.350
1950	El Centro	Sunset	OF	107	369	104	145	25	4	19	108	131	.393*
1951	El Centro/Tijuana	S.W.Int.	OF	116	363	64	114	29	1	19	95	144*	.314
1952	Tijuana	S.W.Int.	OF	123	377	123	138	22	6	28*	131*	180*	.366
	Minor League totals			1333	4477	1339	1566	319	58	284	1313	1666	.350

*Led league

Appendix

Can You Say *Yde*?

BASEBALL PLAYER
PRONUNCIATION GUIDE

Napoleon Lajoie was a tremendous player with a difficult name. I've heard him called "la-JOY," which I know isn't right. (It's probably "LAHJ-away," but some insist on "lahj-WAH.") Other names I've wondered about include Mertes, Bluege, Cicotte, Yde, Luque, and Shaute.

For fun, I began compiling a list of ballplayer pronunciations a couple of years ago while working on this book. I believe this is the first time a guide to pronunciations has been printed. It's a bit of a work in progress, but I don't think there are many mistakes. (My guess is that a few of the names some experts will think are wrong are actually correct. Herm Reich, for instance, does indeed pronounce his name "Rich.")

The pronunciations are from various editions of the *Baseball Register*, occasional newspaper articles, and conversations with writers David Nemec, Joe A. Cronin, and Bob Broeg ("Brayg"), and several former players including Bobby Adams, Dick Adams, Dave Roberts, Gene Desautels, Bernie James, Ray Benge, Joe Hauser, Les Munns, Gus Suhr, Charlie Wallgren, and Dick Bartell.

A "g" in the pronunciation guide is always a hard "g," as in "golf." When two pronunciations are given, the first one is a pronunciation used during the player's career; the second is what is believed to be the proper family pronunciation.

Aase (Don), "AH-see"
Aguirre (Hank), "ah-GEAR-ee"
Aker (Jack), "A-kur"
Alyea (Brant), "ALL-yay"
Amelung (Ed), "AM-uh-lung"
Amoros (Sandy), "AM-or-ohs"
Andujar (Joachin), "AN-du-har"
Arlett (Buzz), "ar-LET"
Avila (Bobby), "ah-VEE-luh"
Ayala (Benny), "eye-AL-uh"

Bacque (Gene), "BAH-kay"
Bacsik (Mike), "BASS-ik"
Baczewski (Fred), "BAH-jess-key"
Baldschun (Jack), "BALL-shun"
Ballou (Win), "buh-LOO"
Bathe (Bill, Bob), "bayth"
Bauman (Joe), "BAU-man"
Baumann (Frank), "BO-man"
Beauchamp (Jim), "BE-chum"
Bedell (Howie), "buh-DELL"
Benge (Ray), "benj"
Bengough (Benny), "ben-GO"
Bernal (Victor), "bur-NAL"
Bernier (Carlos), "bur-NEAR"
Bessent (Don), "buh-SENT"
Blefary (Curt), "BLEF-ah-ree"
Blomberg (Ron), "BLOOM-burg"
Bluege (Ossie, Otto), "BLUE-jee"
Blyzka (Mike), "BLIZZ-kuh"
Bochte (Bruce), "BOCK-tee"
Bochy (Bruce), "BOE-chee"
Boehmer (Len), "BAY-mer"
Bohne (Sammy), "bone"
Boisclair (Bruce), "BO-clair"

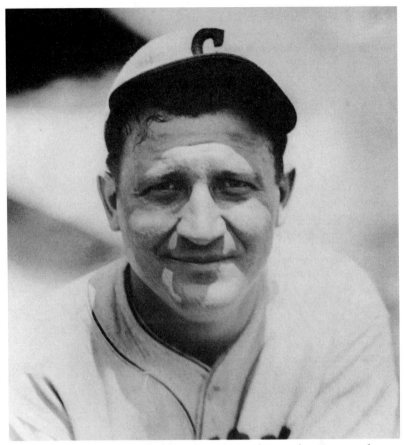

Want to make some money? Convince someone to bet you he can correctly pronounce Joe Shaute's name. A 20-game winner for Cleveland in 1924, Shaute insisted that his name was pronounced "SHAY-oot." (*Courtesy of National Baseball Hall of Fame Library & Archive, Cooperstown, NY*)

Bordagaray (Frenchy), "bor-duh-guh-RAY"
Bouchee (Ed), "boo-SHAY"
Boudreau (Lou), "BOO-dro"; "buh-DRO"
Bourque (Pat), "burk"
Bouton (Jim), "BAU-ton"
Breazeale (Jim), "bruh-ZILL"
Brecheen (Harry), "bruh-KEEN"
Bressoud (Eddie), "bruh-SUE"
Brideweser (Jim), "BRIDE-weez-ur"

Broglio (Ernie), "BRO-lee-o"
Brohamer (Jack), "BRO-hammer"
Brouthers (Dan), "BROO-thurz"
Browne (Pidge), "BROWN-ee"
Brunet (George), "brue-NET"; "brue-NAY"
Burkett (Jesse), "bur-KET"
Burkett (John), "BUR-ket"
Bush (Donie), "bush, DOE-nee"

Cardenal (Jose), "kar-duh-NAHL"
Caveney (Ike), "KAV-en-ee"
Ceccarelli (Art), "chick-are-ELL-ee"
Chakales (Bob), "SHACK-ulls"
Cheney (Tom), "CHAIN-ee"
Cicotte (Al), "SEE-cot"
Cimoli (Gino), "sim-O-lee"; "chim-O-lee"
Combs (Earle), "koombz"
Cottier (Chuck), "KOT-ee-er"
Criger (Lou), "CRIGG-ur"
Critz (Hughie), "crItz" (long *i*, as in *sight*)
Cuellar (Bobby, Mike), "KWAY-arr"

D'Acquisto (John), "DEE-uh-KWISS-toe"
Deas (Pete), "DEE-is"
DeCinces (Doug), "duh-SIN-say"
Dedeaux (Rod), "DEE-doe"
Demeter (Don, Steve), "DEM-it-ur"
Desautels (Gene), "deh-ZUH-tell"
Detore (George), "DEE-tor"
Didier (Bob), "DEE-dee-ay"
Dietz (Dick), "deets"
Dihigo (Martin), "duh-HEE-go, mar-TEEN"
Dilone (Miguel), "dee-loh-NAY"
Douthit (Taylor), "DAU-thit"
Dreisewerd (Clem), "DRIZE-werd"
Dropo (Walt), "DRO-po"
Dubuc (Jean), "duh-BUKE"
Dybzinski (Jerry), "dib-ZIN-skee"
Dyck (Jim), "dike"

Eaddy (Don), "ED-ee"
Epstein (Mike), "EP-steen"
Essegian (Chuck), "uh-SEE-jee-unn"
Evers (Hoot, Joe, Johnny), "EE-verz"

Ferrarese (Don), "ferr-R-see"
Fornieles (Mike), "for-NEE-lis"
Fosse (Ray), "FOSS-ee"
Fournier (Jack), "for-NEAR"
Freisleben (Dave), "FREEZ-leb-en"
Freitas (Tony), "FRAY-tiss"
Frey (Benny), "fry"

Gaedel (Eddie), "guh-DELL"
Galan (Augie), "guh-LANN"
Gentile (Jim), "jen-TEEL"
Giebell (Floyd), "GEE-bil"
Giel (Paul), "geel"
Goetz (Larry, Russ), "getz"
Grba (Eli), "GERB-ah"
Greif (Bill), "grife"
Grote (Jerry), "GROTE-ee"
Groth (Johnny), "growth"
Grzenda (Joe), "greh-ZEN-duh"
Guerra (Mike), "GEHR-uh"
Guisti (Dave), "JUSS-tee"
Guisto (Louie), "GISS-toe"
Gwosdz (Doug), "goosh"

Haak (Howie), "hake"
Haas (Bert, Bruno, Eddie, Mule), "hoss"
Hanebrink (Harry), "HAIN-uh-brink"
Heaverlo (Dave), "HAV-er-low"
Hebert (Billy), "HEE-burt"
Hebert (Wallace), "A-bare"
Heilmann (Harry), "HILE-man"
Heise (Bob), "hise" or "HI-see"
Henrich (Tommy), "HENN-rick"
Hoeft (Billy), "heft"

Horne (Beryln), "horn"
Hough (Charlie), "huff"
Hovley (Steve), "HOVE-lee"
Hrabosky (Al), "ruh-BAH-skee"
Hrbek (Kent), "HUR-beck"
Hriniak (Walt), "RINN-ee-akk"
Huyke (Woody), "HI-kee"

Inao (Kazuhisa), "IN-ow"
Iorg (Dane, Garth), "org"

Judnich (Walt), "JUDD-nick"
Jurges (Billy), "JUR-gez"

Kaat (Jim), "kott"
Katt (Ray), "kott"
Kiely (Leo), "KI-lee"
Kison (Bruce), "KEE-sun"
Knoop (Bobby), "kuh-NOP"
Koenig (Fred, Mark), "KAY-nig"
Konieczny (Doug), "kuh-NEZZ-nee"
Krausse (Lew), "kraus"
Kremer (Ray), "KRAME-er"
Krug (Chris), "kroog"
Kucks (Johnny), "cooks"
Kuehl (Karl), "keel"
Kuenn (Harvey), "keen"
Kusnyer (Art), "KUSH-ner"

Labine (Clem), "luh-BINE"
Lahoud (Joe), "la-WHO"
Lajoie (Napoleon), "LAHJ-away"
Lavagetto (Harry), "lav-uh-JET-oh"
Lavalliere (Mike), "luh-VOLL-yurr"
Lea (Charlie), "lee"
LeBourveau (Bevo), "luh-BOR-vo"
Lefebvre (Jim, Tip), "luh-FEE-ver"
Lefebvre (Joe), "luh-FAY"
Lemanczyk (Dave), "luh-MAN-chick"
Leonhard (Dave), "LEN-ard"

Mike Ryba was one of baseball's most versatile players. A catcher, first baseman, third baseman, outfielder, and pitcher, he led the Western League in hitting in 1933 (.380 for the St. Louis Cardinals' Springfield team) and later became a 20-game winner for Columbus and Rochester. He also sold tickets, managed, and worked in the front office before he reached the majors. The Pennsylvania native pronounced his name "REE-buh." (© *Brace Photo*)

Liddle (Don), "LID-ul"
Lien (Al), "leen"
Lipon (Johnny), "LIPP-on"
Llenas (Winston), "YAY-nuss"
Lodigiani (Dario), "lo-duh-JONN-ee"
Lolich (Mickey, Ron), "LO-lich"
Lonnett (Joe), "lon-ETT"
Lown (Turk), "lown" (rhymes with *town*)
Lucchesi (Frank), "loo-CASE-ee"
Luque (Adolfo), "LOO-kay"

Mackiewicz (Felix), "MACK-uh-wits"
Maisel (Fritz, George), "MY-zell"
Malzone (Frank), "mal-ZONE"
Mamaux (Al), "ma-MOO"
Manush (Frank, Heinie), "man-OOSH"
Marchildon (Phil), "MAR-shill-dun"
Mauch (Gene), "mock"
McGaha (Mel), "muh-GAY-uh"
Mejias (Roman), "muh-HEE-us"
Mele (Al, Sam), "MEE-lee"
Mertes (Sam), "MURR-teez"
Minarcin (Rudy), "min-ARR-sin"
Monge (Sid), "MON-guh"
Monteagudo (Aurelio, Rene), "mon-TEE-ah-GOO-doe"
Montemayor (Felipe), "monn-tuh-MY-or, fuh-LEE-pay"
Moret (Rogelio), "mor-A, roe-HEE-lee-o"
Mostil (Johnny), "MOSS-till"

Necciai (Ron), "NETCH-eye"
Neun (Johnny), "noon"
Niarhos (Gus), "NYE-ur-hoss"
Niehoff (Bert), "NEE-hoff"
Noble (Ray), "NO-blay"

Oeschger (Joe), "ESH-gur"

Paciorek (Jim, John, Mike, Tom), "pah-CHORR-ik"
Paepke (Dennis, Jack), "PAPP-key"
Pagan (Dave, Jose), "puh-GONN"

Palica (Bo, Erv), "pah-LEE-kuh"
Palys (Stan), "PAL-iss"
Passeau (Claude), "pass-O"
Patek (Freddie), "PAW-tek"
Pavletich (Don), "pav-LET-ik"
Peckinpaugh (Roger), "PECK-in-paw"
Petrocelli (Rico), "pet-roh-CHELL-ee"
Phillippe (Deacon), "fuh-LEEP"
Phoebus (Tom), "FEE-bus"
Picciolo (Rob), "PEACH-uh-low"
Piche (Ron), "pee-SHAY"
Picinich (Val), "pah-SIN-itch"
Pilarcik (Al), "pill-R-sick"
Pillette (Duane, Herman), "pill-ETT"
Pocoroba (Biff), "poh-kuh-ROH-buh"
Podgajny (Johnny), "puh-JONN-ee"
Poepping (Mike), "PEP-ping"
Pollett (Howie), "pul-LETT"
Ponce (Carlos, Tony), "PONE-say"
Posedel (Bill), "poze-DELL"
Power (Victor Pellot), "POW-urr, VEEK-tor pay-UTT"
Pytlak (Frankie), "PIT-lack"

Radatz (Dick), "RAD-itz"
Rajsich (Dave, Gary), "RAY-sitch"
Rakow (Ed), "ROCK-oh"
Rauch (Bob), "rock"
Raymond (Claude), "ruh-MONE"
Reich (Herm), "rich"
Reichardt (Rick), "RYE-kart"
Remy (Jerry), "REMM-ee"
Reuschel (Paul, Rick), "RUSH-ull"
Reuss (Jerry), "royce"
Riebe (Hank), "REE-bee"
Roenicke (Gary, Ron), "RENN-uh-key"
Roettger (Oscar, Wally), "RUTT-gur"
Rogell (Billy), "roe-GELL"
Rojek (Stan), "ROE-jack"
Rozema (Dave), "ROSE-muh"
Ruhle (Vern), "rule"

Runge (Ed, Paul), "RUNN-gee"
Ryba (Mike), "REE-buh"

Sadek (Mike), "SAY-deck"
Saffell (Tom), "SAFF-ful"
Saier (Vic), "seer" (rhymes with *near*)
Salmon (Chico), "suh-MONE"
Sanguillen (Manny), "san-GEE-en"
Saucier (Frank), "so-SHAY"
Schaal (Paul), "shawl"
Schaive (Johnny), "SHY-vee"
Scharein (George), "shar-on"
Scheinblum (Richie), "SHINE-bloom"
Schoendienst (Paul, Red), "SCHANE-deenst"
Scull (Angel), "skool"
Secory (Frank), "suh-KOR-ee"
Seghi (Phil), "SEE-gee"
Segui (David, Diego), "suh-GEE"
Serena (Bill), "suh-REEN-uh"
Shaute (Joe), "SHAY-oot"
Show (Eric), "shau"
Sleater (Lou), "SLATE-ur"
Solaita (Tony), "soh-LEE-tuh"
Stange (Lee), "stang"
Starrette (Herm), "stah-RET"
Staub (Rusty), "stobb"
Stubing (Moose), "STEW-bing"
Sudakis (Bill), "suh-DAY-kis"
Sukeforth (Clyde), "SUE-kuh-forth"
Susce (George), "SUE-see"
Sutter (Bruce), "SUE-ter"
Szekely (Joe), "ZECK-lee"

Tappe (Elvin, Ted), "TAPP-ee"
Tesreau (Jeff), "TEZ-roe"
Teufel (Tim), "TUFF-ull"
Thies (Dave, Jake) "tees"
Tiefenauer (Bobby), "tee-fen-AU-er"
Tighe (Jack), "tie"

Tost (Lou), "toast"
Tracewski (Dick), "truh-ZOO-skee"
Trouppe (Quincy), "troop"
Tsitouris (Johnny), "suh-TORR-iss"

Uecker (Bob), "YOO-kur"
Uhlaender (Ted), "YOO-lann-der"
Uhle (George), "YOO-lee"

Valo (Elmer), "VOLL-oh"
Vergez (Johnny), "VIR-jes"
Versalles (Zoilo), "vur-ZIE-yez, ZOE-lo"
Veryzer (Tom), "ver-EYE-zer"
Viox (Jim), "VEE-ox"

Wagner (Honus), "WAG-ner, HONN-iss"
Warneke (Lon), "wor-NUH-kee"
Weik (Dick), "wike"
Weiland (Bob), "WHY-lund"
Weis (Al, Art), "whyss"
Werle (Bill), "whirl"
Weyhing (Gus, John), "WAY-ing"
Whitted (Possum), "WHITE-ed"
Wiesler (Bob), "WEEZ-lur"
Wietelmann (Whitey), "WEE-tull-man"
Witte (Jerry), "WITT-ee"

Yde (Emil), "EE-dee"
Yochim (Len, Ray), "YO-kum"
Yost (Ed, Ned), "yoast"
Yvars (Sal), "EE-varz"

Zauchin (Norm), "ZOW-chin"
Zdeb (Joe), "zeb"

Raised on an Arkansas farm, pitcher Lon Warneke pitched 13 full major-league seasons, winning 193 games while losing only 121. He won 20 games three times for the Cubs, and finished his career with a sparkling 3.18 ERA. A singer and guitar player in the St. Louis Cardinals' Mudcat Band, Warneke later umpired before becoming a judge in Arkansas. (© *Brace Photo*)

INDEX